Twayne's English Authors Series

Sylvia E. Bowman, *Editor*

INDIANA UNIVERSITY

E. M. Forster

(TEAS) 89

E. M. Forster

By FREDERICK P. W. McDOWELL

University of Iowa

TWAYNE PUBLISHERS

A DIVISION OF G. K. HALL & CO., BOSTON

Contents

Preface

ACCORDING to Arnold Bennett in 1910, E. M. Forster was the most discussed writer of the year because of the sensation he produced among the intelligentsia with *Howards End*. Bennett was apprehensive for Forster because a writer who had published four arresting novels in five years might be tempted to exploit his success and become merely "fashionable." Instead, Forster followed the alternative course which Bennett suggested: "If, on the other hand, he writes solely to please himself, forgetting utterly the existence of the *élite*, he may produce some first-class literature." [1] The "first-class literature" Forster wrote thereafter was not voluminous: *A Passage to India* (1924) and several miscellaneous volumes.

World War I deflected Forster from his career as novelist and shocked him spiritually. He served as a volunteer officer with the Red Cross in Egypt from 1915 to 1919 and recorded his impressions in *Alexandria: A History and a Guide* (1922) and in *Pharos and Pharillon* (1923). After the war he wrote mostly essays and reviews, but a second trip to India in 1921 inspired him to complete *A Passage to India*, begun in 1913. Public and critics acclaimed *A Passage to India*, and this book re-established him as an important writer. All the novels were republished in England in 1924, and most were reprinted or published for the first time in America in the 1920's. Interest in Forster was keen during the 1920's, but it leveled off in the 1930's.

As if he were following Bennett's counsel, Forster wrote to please himself. He discovered, however, that the social world he had known was no longer firm; and his humanistic values, strong enough for him to live by, were insufficient to support him in major creative efforts. [2] He was not able, therefore, to depict in fiction a milieu that had grown strange to him. [3] Postwar Europe repudiated, at least in part, the values he had cherished; or it embraced values alien to him. Forster's miscellaneous work in the 1930's and later broadened his range, extended his authority, and increased his stature as a man of letters, however disappointing his abandoning the novel may have been. In this writing he expressed many ideas and attitudes present in his fiction or current versions of them.

In the 1930's Forster remained an influence, more as a critic perhaps than as an artist. His voice became increasingly public, as the menace at home and abroad to intellectual freedom and democratic institutions became sharper. By World War II Forster had become a spokesman for the cultivated public and the intelligentsia alike with his protests against domestic conformity and Nazi tyranny in *The Nordic Twilight,* in the broadcast talks based on this book, and in numerous other utterances. Forster's values were, in the main, still those of nineteenth-century Romanticism, liberalism, and humanism. Although Forster loomed largest as a public figure in the late 1930's and early 1940's, he achieved some recognition for his fiction in Rose Macaulay's *The Writings of E. M. Forster* and in F. R. Leavis' essay-review of it in *Scrutiny,* both 1938.

With the publication of Lionel Trilling's *E. M. Forster* (1943) the present "Forster revival" began. Trilling's book, for all its brilliance, has the faults of a pioneer work. It is sometimes reductive in its analyses and expeditious in its judgments. Trilling's authoritative manner and Leavis' forthright judgments inhibited other critics, for a time, from writing on Forster. Consequently, no other extended treatise appeared until James McConkey's *The Novels of E. M. Forster* (1957).

McConkey's book inaugurated a renaissance in Forster criticism. Between 1943 and 1957 few articles on Forster had appeared, and Rex Warner's 1953 pamphlet in the "Writers and Their Work" series had been the only survey made of Forster's work. After 1957 articles became ubiquitous: interpretive bibliographies of the criticism were compiled in *English Fiction in Transition,* a Forster issue of *Modern Fiction Studies* came out in 1960, and B. J. Kirkpatrick's bibliography of Forster's work appeared in 1965. Since 1960 thirteen general books on Forster have been written. Most of them have value, and those by Beer, Crews, Stone, and Thomson, are authoritative. The novels have been issued in paperback in England and America, and the English Pocket Edi-

Preface

tion is still in print. In the 1960's the popularity of Forster's books and the volume of the critical work he has inspired have established him as a major artist, intellectual voice, and man of letters.

FREDERICK P. W. McDOWELL

University of Iowa

Acknowledgments

I AM indebted to the Old Gold Foundation and the Graduate College of the University of Iowa for providing me with a summer fellowship to work on this book. The Graduate College of the University of Iowa also provided me with funds for the duplication of printed materials and for typing my manuscript. Over the years Professor John C. Gerber, Head of the Department of English at the University of Iowa, has encouraged me with this study as have my colleagues on the Modern Letters faculty at the University of Iowa. I owe much also to my wife for her judicious appraisal of my work at various stages and for her continued interest in my book.

Acknowledgment is made to Edward Arnold Ltd. for permission to reprint from these books by E. M. Forster: *Where Angels Fear to Tread, The Longest Journey, A Room with a View, Howards End, A Passage to India, Aspects of the Novel, Goldsworthy Lowes Dickinson, Abinger Harvest, Two Cheers for Democracy, The Hill of Devi,* and *Marianne Thornton.*

Acknowledgment is made to Alfred A. Knopf, Inc. for permission to reprint from these books by E. M. Forster: *Where Angels Fear to Tread, The Longest Journey, A Room with a View, Howards End,* and *Pharos and Pharillon.*

Acknowledgment is made to Harcourt, Brace and World, Inc. to reprint from these books by E. M. Forster: *A Passage to India, Aspects of the Novel, Goldsworthy Lowes Dickinson, Abinger Harvest, Two Cheers for Democracy, The Hill of Devi,* and *Marianne Thornton;* also from *E. M. Forster: A Tribute,* edited by K. Natwar-Singh (1964).

Doubleday and Company, Inc. has granted permission to reprint from E. M. Forster's *Alexandria: A History and a Guide.*

The Hogarth Press Ltd. has granted permission to reprint from E. M. Forster's *England's Pleasant Land* and his "Notes for a

Reply" in Julian Bell, *Essays, Poems and Letters*, edited by Quentin Bell (1938).

The Oxford University Press has granted permission to reprint from E. M. Forster's "Introduction" to the World's Classics edition of *The Longest Journey* (1960).

Methuen and Company Ltd. has granted permission to reprint from E. M. Forster's "Preface" to Goldsworthy Lowes Dickinson's *The Greek View of Life* (23rd edition; 1957).

Pantheon Books (Random House, Inc.) and The Harvill Press Ltd. have granted permission to reprint from E. M. Forster's "Introduction" to Giuseppe di Lampedusa's *Two Stories and a Memory* (trans. by Archibald Colquhoun, 1962).

Curtis Brown Ltd. and Charles Scribner's Sons have granted permission to reprint from E. M. Forster's "Introduction" to Donald Windham's *The Warm Country* (1960).

George Allen and Unwin Ltd. has granted permission to reprint from E. M. Forster's "Some Memories" in *Edward Carpenter: An Appreciation*, edited by Gilbert Beith (1931).

E. M. Forster and the editors of the appropriate periodicals have granted permission to reprint from his uncollected articles as follows:

"The Long Run," *New Statesman and Nation* (December 19, 1938).

"The Charm and Strength of Mrs. Gaskell," *Sunday Times* (April 7, 1957).

Letter from E. M. Forster, *Griffin*, I (1951; published by Readers' Subscription, Inc.).

"More Browning Letters" (October 13, 1938), "Freedom for What" (June 1, 1939), "My Poultry Are Not Officers" (October 26, 1939), "The Individual and His God" (December 5, 1940), "A Clash of Authority" (June 22, 1944), " 'In the Rue Lepsius' " (July 5, 1951), "The Art and Architecture of India" (September 10, 1953), "The World Mountain" (December 2, 1954), "The Blue Boy" (March 14, 1957), *Listener*.

"Indian Entries from a Diary," *Harper's Magazine* (February, 1962); "Indian Entries," *Encounter* (January, 1962).

Editorial, *London Times* (January 1, 1958).

For permission to reprint from other copyrighted books, acknowledgment is made to the following:

Acknowledgments

The British Council for Rex Warner's *E. M. Forster* (Writers and Their Work, No. 7, 1964 edition).

J. M. Dent and Sons Ltd. for Peter Burra's "Introduction" to Everyman's Library edition of *A Passage to India* (1942).

Wayne State University Press for George H. Thomson's *The Fiction of E. M. Forster* (1967).

Cornell University Press for James McConkey's *The Novels of E. M. Forster* (1957).

Stanford University Press for Wilfred Stone's *The Cave and the Mountain* (1966).

A. P. Watt and Son (Hastings House), Greenwood Press, Inc., Doubleday and Company, Inc., and Mrs. D. Cheston Bennett for Arnold Bennett's *Books and Persons* (1917).

Chatto and Windus Ltd. for E. B. C. Jones, "E. M. Forster and Virginia Woolf" in *The English Novelists* (1936), edited by Derek Verschoyle.

Chatto and Windus Ltd. and New York University for F. R. Leavis' *The Common Pursuit* (1952).

New York University Press for Alan Wilde's *Art and Order: A Study of E. M. Forster* (1964).

Princeton University Press for Frederick C. Crews's *E. M. Forster: The Perils of Humanism* (1962).

For permission to reprint from the following articles, acknowledgment is made to the editor of the appropriate periodical:

Modern Fiction Studies © 1961 by Purdue Research Foundation, Lafayette, Indiana, for Frederick J. Hoffman's "*Howards End* and the Bogey of Progress," VII (1961); John Magnus' "Ritual Aspects of E. M. Forster's *The Longest Journey*," XIII (1967); and Frederick P. W. McDowell's "Forster's 'Natural Supernaturalism': The Tales," VII (1961).

Critical Quarterly for Malcolm Bradbury's "E. M. Forster's *Howards End*," IV (1962).

Critique for Frederick P. W. McDowell's "Forster's Many-Faceted Universe: Idea and Paradox in *The Longest Journey*," IV (1960–61).

Encounter for Angus Wilson's "A Conversation with E. M. Forster," IX (November, 1957).

For permission to reprint from John Crowe Ransom's "E. M. Forster" (1943), acknowledgment is made to Mr. Ransom and to the editor of the *Kenyon Review*.

For permission to reprint from Frederick P. W. McDowell's " 'The Mild Intellectual Light': Idea and Theme in *Howards End*," *PMLA*, LXXIV (1959), acknowledgment is made to the Modern Language Association of America.

Chronology

1879	January 1: Edward Morgan Forster born in London. October: death of father, Edward Morgan Llewellyn Forster.
1887	November: death of Marianne Thornton, aunt, who left Forster legacy of 8,000 pounds.
ca. 1883– ca. 1893	Life at Hertfordshire home, prototype of "Howards End."
ca. 1890– ca. 1892	Educated at preparatory school, Eastbourne.
ca. 1893– ca. 1901	Life at Tonbridge and Tonbridge Wells.
1893– 1897	Educated as day-boy, Tonbridge School.
1897– 1901	Matriculation, King's College, Cambridge. Came under influence of Goldsworthy Lowes Dickinson, J. M. E. McTaggart, Roger Fry, and especially Nathaniel Wedd, his Classics tutor.
1900	Bachelor of Arts Degree, Second Class in Classical Tripos, Part I. Studied under Nathaniel Wedd.
1901	Bachelor of Arts Degree, Second Class in Historical Tripos, Part II. Studied under Oscar Browning.
1901– 1902	Travel in Italy and Greece; residence in Italy.
ca. 1902– ca. 1945	Residence at Abinger Hammer, Surrey.
1903	Contributed "Albergo Empedocle," first short story, to *Temple Bar*. Goldsworthy Lowes Dickinson, G. M. Trevelyan, Nathaniel Wedd, Edward Jenks, and others founded *Independent Review*. Began *A Room with a View*.
1903– 1908	Contributed essays and short stories to *Independent Review*.

1905   *Where Angels Fear to Tread.*

1907   *The Longest Journey.*

1908   *A Room with a View.* Began work on *Howards End.*

1910   *Howards End* published in London and New York. Master of Arts Degree, King's College, Cambridge.

1911   *The Celestial Omnibus and Other Stories. A Room with a View* published in America.

1912–
1913   October to March: first visit to India, with Goldsworthy Lowes Dickinson and R. C. Trevelyan. Sojourn included visit to Maharajah of Dewas State Senior.

1913   Began work on *A Passage to India.*

1914   Wrote essays and reviews for *New Weekly.*

1915–
1919   November, 1915, to January, 1919: volunteer officer with Red Cross at Alexandria, Egypt.

1919–
1920   Literary editor of *Daily Herald.*

1920   *Where Angels Fear to Tread* published in America. *The Story of the Siren.*

1921   March to October: second visit to India as private secretary to Maharajah of Dewas State Senior. Presented with Tukyjirao Gold Medal. *Howards End* reissued in America.

1922   *Alexandria: A History and a Guide. The Longest Journey* published in America.

1922–
1923   Further work on *A Passage to India.*

1923   *Pharos and Pharillon* published in Richmond and New York. *A Room with a View* reissued in America. *The Celestial Omnibus and Other Stories* published in America.

1924   *A Passage to India* published in London and New York. Novels reissued.

1925   Received Femina Vie Heureuse and James Tait Black Memorial Prizes for *A Passage to India.*

1927   Elected Fellow, King's College, Cambridge. Delivered Clark Lectures, auspices of Trinity College; published as *Aspects of the Novel* in London and New York.

1928   *The Eternal Moment and Other Stories* published in London and New York.

1934   *Goldsworthy Lowes Dickinson* published in London

and New York. "The Abinger Pageant" produced at Abinger Hammer.

1934– First president of National Council for Civil Liberties.
1935 Again president in 1942; resigned, 1948.
1936 *Abinger Harvest: A Miscellany* published in London and New York.
1940 *Nordic Twilight* and *England's Pleasant Land, A Pageant Play.*
1941 *Virginia Woolf: The Rede Lecture.*
1943 Lionel Trilling's *E. M. Forster* and republishing of novels in America by Knopf and New Directions inaugurated "Forster revival."
1944 Trilling's *E. M. Forster* published in London.
1945 *The Development of English Prose between 1918 and 1939* (The Ker Lecture).
October-December: third visit to India to attend P.E.N. Conference at Jaipur.
ca. 1945 to present Residence at Cambridge; Honorary Fellow, King's College.
1947 Visit to United States to address "The Symposium on Music Criticism" at Harvard University, May 1–3; lectured on "The Raison d'Etre of Criticism in the Arts." Uniform Pocket Edition of novels published. *The Collected Tales of E. M. Forster* published in America.
1948 *The Collected Short Stories of E. M. Forster* published in England.
1949 Second visit to United States to address American Academy of Arts and Letters for annual presentation of awards; lectured on "Art for Art's Sake," May 27.
1950 Dramatization of *A Room with a View* by S. Tait and K. Allott, Cambridge.
1951 *Two Cheers for Democracy* published in London and New York. Honorary Doctor of Letters Degree, Nottingham University.
1952 *Billy Budd* published in London and New York (opera adapted with Eric Crozier for Benjamin Britten from the story by Herman Melville).
1953 Named to membership in Order of Companions of Honor to the Queen; received and invested by Queen

Elizabeth II, February 13. *The Hill of Devi* published in London and New York.

1956   *Marianne Thornton: A Domestic Biography* published in London and New York.

1960   Dramatization of *A Passage to India* by Santha Rama Rau at Oxford; London run, April 20–December 3.

1961   *Alexandria: A History and a Guide* published in America with introduction by E. M. Forster. Named Companion of Literature by Royal Society of Literature, May 10.

1962   Dramatization of *A Passage to India;* New York run, January 31–May 10.

1963–   Dramatization of *Where Angels Fear to Tread* by Eliza-
1964   beth Hart; London run, July 9, 1963–January 25, 1964.

1967   Dramatization of *Howards End* by Lance Sieveking and Richard Cotrell; London run, February 28–April 1.

1969   January 1: appointed member of Order of Merit by Queen Elizabeth II.

Ninetieth birthday; and publication in London and New York of *Aspects of E. M. Forster: Essays and Recollections Written for His Ninetieth Birthday January 1, 1969,* edited by Oliver Stallybrass.

CHAPTER 1

E. M. Forster: Writer, Moralist, and Thinker

I Humanism and Cambridge

IN 1938 when a new world war threatened, Forster began to feel that all was lost "except personal affection, the variety of human conduct, the importance of truth."[1] All else had been lost except this humanistic ideal and it seemed now to be in peril. Only "the fag end" of that Victorian liberalism remained in which his humanism was rooted; and he was anxious that this much, at least, of a vital tradition survive in the difficult days ahead. In 1941, celebrating the hundredth anniversary of the London Library, Forster defined a laudable aim in terms of an individualistic altruistic humanism that was published in *Two Cheers for Democracy*: "the desire to know more, the desire to feel more, and . . . the desire to help others" (305).* Intelligence, emotional sensitivity, and humanitarian sympathy—such are the attributes of temper to which Forster has given his allegiance.

The humanism which Forster defended in the 1930's and the 1940's had its origins in many strands of eighteenth- and nineteenth-century culture. Forster was an eclectic, deriving his ideas from varied sources; he admits in *Aspects of the Novel* his eclecticism at the same time that he disparages the hit and miss action of the human mind (147). In "Battersea Rise" of *Abinger Harvest*, in "Henry Thornton" of *Two Cheers for Democracy*, and in the biography of Marianne Thornton, his aunt, he depicted the milieu of his maternal ancestors, as characterized by evangelicism, moral responsibility, and Utilitarian liberalism in politics. Forster, the moralist, derived in part from the Clapham sect to which these ancestors of his belonged; his democratic instincts can likewise be traced to their orthodox Utilitarianism.[2] John Stuart Mill's modifications of Utilitarianism in the direction of a democratic socialism were more attractive to Forster than to the Thorntons who, as

* See Selected Bibliography, Primary Sources, for texts used; they are indicated with an asterisk.

businessmen, distrusted government intervention in the country's economy.

Other forces converged upon Forster during his Cambridge days (1897–1901). The idealism, humanitarianism, and nature worship of romanticists like Wordsworth, Shelley, and Meredith were congenial. The prophets of the Victorian Age—Carlyle, Ruskin, Arnold, and William Morris—influenced him with their subjectively derived values, their realistic appraisals of social life, their indignation at man's inhumanity to man, and their moral conscientiousness. The Christian idealism of nineteenth-century intellectuals and the theological skepticism of men like Matthew Arnold and Leslie Stephen were also shaping pressures; and enthusiasm for Classical literature and culture resulted from contact with his tutor Nathaniel Wedd.

The Cambridge experience is the most important in Forster's career. What Cambridge meant to him we can infer from the opening chapters of *The Longest Journey* and from recollections recorded in *Goldsworthy Lowes Dickinson*. In *The Longest Journey*, Cambridge ministers to the tormented Rickie Elliot after an unhappy youth at a day school similar to Sawston at which he later teaches. So for Forster Cambridge emanated sweetness and light after his alienated years at Tonbridge School and restored some of the equanimity he had known as a child with his mother and great-aunt in Hertfordshire and Clapham Common.

In his biography of Dickinson, Forster enlarged upon the revelation that Cambridge brought to his friend and mentor. It taught him, Forster said, that the world of the public school is not eternal; that there is activity more engaging than "teamwork"; that there are attributes more appealing than "firmness, self-complacency and fatuity"; that intellectual endeavor may be a pleasure as well as a task; and that personal freedom is in large part a result of one's unaided efforts (26). Such a revelation came to Forster as well as to Dickinson. On the credit side, Cambridge expanded Forster's view of human possibilities. On the debit side, it may have encouraged a culture somewhat too bloodless and self-contained, a culture—like Bloomsbury's—centered mostly in the preferences of the individual and in the exercise of reason.

At Cambridge, Forster came to know Dickinson and, through the Midnight Society and the Apostles discussion group, such men as Leonard Woolf, Lytton Strachey, John Maynard Keynes, Desmond MacCarthy, Clive Bell, Thoby Stephen, Roger Fry, and Saxon Sydney-Turner, who were later in London to form the nucleus of the Bloomsbury Group. In addition to these men, Virginia Woolf, Vanessa Bell (her sister), Adrian Stephen (her brother), and Duncan Grant were associated with this group in the years before World War I and after.[3] Indirectly through his associations at Cambridge or through his loose affiliations with Bloomsbury, Forster also assimilated some of G. E. Moore's concepts, in particular the idea that the highest good derives in part from personal relationships and in part from esthetic perceptions.

Above all else, Cambridge developed in Forster the temper of the humanist. Just what this temper meant to Forster many of his incidental statements reveal: his assertion that spontaneity, variety, and complexity are the marks of a true culture; his conviction that "tolerance, good temper and sympathy" need strengthening even if they are not entirely effective weapons in the modern world; and his view that early Christianity, under Clement, had an intellectual distinction, persuasiveness, and graciousness lacking in the more extreme doctrines of Athanasius.[4]

In an interview in 1947, Forster confessed indebtedness to the thought and temper of Matthew Arnold.[5] Even without this statement, we would suspect that affinities do exist between the two. Arnold might have been speaking for Forster when he cited the powers which human nature must develop before a true culture can prevail: "the power of conduct . . . the power of intellect and knowledge, the power of beauty, the power of social life and manners."[6] To some such complex of standards—intellectual, esthetic, personal, and ethical—Forster remained loyal. When, during the Spanish Civil War, Julian Bell challenged him as to the adequacy of his liberalism, Forster replied that he was unable to change the habits of sixty years and that he would continue to be "gentle, semi-idealistic and semi-cynical, kind, tolerant, demure" —in short, a liberal and a humanist.[7] His humanism was more, then, than a habit of mind; it became a strengthening personal and ethical philosophy during a time of international upheaval.

II *The "Junction of Mind with Heart"*

Like Matthew Arnold before him, Forster is an advocate of reason who recognizes the provenance of intuition. Revealing some indebtedness to romantic theories of symbolism, Forster discovers

a supernal, ineffable sheen which illuminates the perceptions of
the senses. In his non-fiction Forster emphasizes the importance of
this transcendent effluence by exposing the incompleteness of
those who deny it. The religion of the English—Forster asserts in
"Notes on the English Character" in *Abinger Harvest*—is practical, decent, and centered on right conduct, but it lacks the in-
wardness and fervor of an authentic religion (10). The Clapham
sect had no sense of the poetic, let alone of the immanent, Forster
repeated in *Marianne Thornton* (38, 52), in "Battersea Rise," and
in "Henry Thornton."

Forster asserted in 1940 that mankind is engaged in an inner—
or religious—struggle as well as an outer—or political—one, in "a
struggle for truer values, a struggle of the individual towards the
dark, secret place where he may find reality." [8] To such an endeavor to reach reality, Forster constantly bent his own energies.[9]
The irradiation which may result from such an effort, Forster
thinks, is religious because it expresses our sense of identity with a
transcendent power. Forster, in fact, expresses sympathy at times
with Platonism, when, for example, he discusses Constance Sit-
well's *Flowers and Elephants*.[10] In her view, Forster said, each
object grasped by the senses hints at its own absent perfection, its
own essence which may be divine. To their detriment, then, some
intellectuals like H. G. Wells lack all realization that the world
defined by the senses may be illusory and that behind the veil of
our impressions may dwell the unalterable. A lack of such intuitive insight, Forster suggests, may result in distortion of actual
fact; for a writer like Wells, aware only of surface phenomena, is
unable to fit them into any enlarged perspective.[11]

The religious aspiration to encounter the Unseen links with
other forms of aspiration, so that, as Forster expresses it in *Goldsworthy Lowes Dickinson* (88, 120), all the arts at their most intense and culture at its most sincere provide opportunities for us
to reach the profoundest truth about the spirit. Dickinson was so
responsive to the creative imagination and so aware of a transcendent realm that he could adopt the long view and remain
unperturbed by both the victories and the defeats of reason. Basic
to Forster's view of experience is his conviction that the enlightened imagination, such as Dickinson possessed, must modulate
the inner and outer lives, and establish a vital interplay between
them. The individual and his society will be organically whole

and sound, then, to the degree that a tolerant perceptiveness determines ethical, social, and philosophical values—values which may have their basis in fact but which thereafter may veer toward the intangible. The intellectual in the distance—Mr. Emerson, Tony Failing, Ernst Schlegel, and Cyril Fielding—is frequently the character most aware of the importance of intuitive sympathy, of the need for imaginative transplantation into the identity of others, and of the value of observing measure and proportion. Fielding, of course, has much less of the mystical than Forster's usual humanist.

Forster, like D. H. Lawrence, recognized the strength of spontaneous impulse and of the passions. As his Bloomsbury affiliation suggests, Forster was more self-conscious and intellectual than Lawrence; but he was also more attracted to the prophetic and to the unconscious than were his London associates. In his judgments of people, Forster, as he has said, is kind to those whose innate feelings are clear and positive; looking back upon the Italians in his fiction, for example, he finds in them, as he remarked to Angus Wilson, "a graciousness that leads into grace" (55). Members of the convention-clad middle class possess little of this instinctive faith in life and in themselves ("animal faith" in the words of Austin Warren[12]). As Forster describes the typical Englishman in "Notes on the English Character" in *Abinger Harvest,* he is more highly developed in mind and body than in heart, and he lacks not so much the capacity as the inclination to respond intuitively (5–8). Mrs. Miniver, in *Two Cheers for Democracy* (299), epitomizes this spiritual dryness in the contemporary middle class. She embodies a conformity and superficial pleasantness from which true distinction, all sense of "spontaneity, natural gaiety, recklessness," is absent.

Granted that intuition enables us to apprehend the more significant values, nevertheless the informed reason alone defines them with exactness. According to Elizabeth Bowen in *Collected Impressions,* intellect balances rather than controls "susceptibility" in Forster's world, and it "edits" feeling (121–23). Intellect is subservient to passion, but passion falsifies when it is undisciplined by the intellect. In describing in 1960 the composition of *The Longest Journey,* Forster remembers how he had attained just such a fusion of his powers, that "junction of mind with heart where the creative impulse sparks." [13]

In an uncollected essay of 1925, "Peeping at Elizabeth," Forster professes his respect for the critical intellect. In the days of Elizabeth, he says, there was little thought, just as there was "little unashamed or uncontorted passion." The age would have gained if its great men had more consistently exercised their minds because, if "thought may betray a man individually and bring Empires to ruin, it is nevertheless the only known preservative, the only earnest of immortality." [14] Writing of Kipling, Forster cites as his chief limitation an intellectual immaturity similar to that he finds in the Elizabethans. The innate capacity of the mind to synthesize—the desire to digest, compare, generalize—and to deduce represents for Forster the most impressive aspect of human activity; and Kipling only sparingly illustrated any such tendency toward disinterested thought.[15]

Eliot in his poetry, on the contrary, steadily deepened his powers, as his reason mellowed and ordered with authority his insights.[16] And in discussing Golding's *Lord of the Flies*, Forster champions the constructive intelligence represented in Piggy, intelligence as it relates to the moral and spiritual enlargement of the race. Through this character Golding conveys his sense of human reason feeling its way, his hope that it may survive and influence events, and his fears that it may not succeed in so doing.[17]

Precisely because Forster sought a supple balance between the rational and the irrational, he emerges as one of those profounder humanists he describes Dickinson as having been, a man who perceived "the importance and the unimportance of reason" (120).

III *"Only Connect": Life's Dichotomies*

From the beginning Forster's values have been ambivalent. As we have seen, respect for lucid intelligence, as it grapples with the realm of fact, opposes an intimation, basic to Romanticism, that an ineffable realm lies just beyond the world perceived by the senses. Two main strands in Forster's mind become evident: the rational, skeptical, logical, or Apollonian; and the intuitive, religious, imaginative, or Dionysian.[18] These tendencies form the basis of contrasting humanisms dramatized in the novels: Mrs. Moore's versus Fielding's in *A Passage to India*, Stephen Wonham's versus Stewart Ansell's in *The Longest Journey*. Characters like Rickie Elliot, Margaret Schlegel, and Professor Godbole unite, with varying success, both ranges of experience. In his fiction Forster charts, accordingly, the relationships between secular experience and mystical aspiration, between the tangible and the intangible, between the empirically observed and the transcendentally poetic.

Forster continually explored life's dichotomies and their reconciliation within the larger framework of the sensibility. A realization of the complexities and gradations in experience was a principal revelation for him at Cambridge. There a "magic fusion" of opposing but complementary entities took place for him no less than for Dickinson:

> Body and spirit, reason and emotion, work and play, architecture and scenery, laughter and seriousness, life and art—these pairs which are everywhere contrasted were there fused into one. People and books reinforced one another, intelligence joined hands with affection, speculation became a passion, and discussion was made profound by love. (35)

Writing of Dickinson twenty years later, Forster just as emphatically asserted that Greek literature, which Forster came to know well at Cambridge, most cogently unifies our perceptions, "beauty and depth, wisdom and wit, gaiety and insight, speculation and ecstasy, carnality and spirit." [19]

A view of life which acknowledges its many sides appealed alike to Dickinson and Forster. Though Forster had no great affection for Goethe, he saw why Goethe enthralled Dickinson: the German's ranging intellect meant that his mental perspectives were infinite, his sympathies generous (45–48). Then, by studying Plato's dialogues, Dickinson sharpened his sense of dialectic: his ability to see the other side of a question and to state it fairly. In short, Dickinson was able to mediate between polarities, to avoid extremes, and to seek a vital center of harmonized impulses. Dickinson and Forster himself resemble the ranging Rickie Elliot of *The Longest Journey* or the enterprising Margaret Schlegel of *Howards End* in a compulsion to embrace as much of experience as possible and to accommodate opposing forces. Margaret, especially, seeks for that unity of which Dante, in Forster's view, dreamed in his conception of an earthly paradise. In defining his vision, Dante was able to discriminate "between the forces that make men alike and the forces that make men different—between the centripetal power that may lead to monotony, and the centrifugal power that may lead to war. These powers are reconciled in the orbits of the stars; and Dante's first and last word to us is that we should imitate the celestial harmony." [20]

Such achievement of proportion must be a creative act, the incremental result of our relative and partial experiences; and the unity to be attained is provisional, not absolutistic. Thus Helen Schlegel fails to win stability until the concluding chapter of *Howards End* because in Platonic fashion she makes an absolute of the spirit and too easily proclaims her affirmations. Nor can the Wilcoxes achieve proportion because they are convention-bound and make absolutes of the values they have derived from a narrow tradition. In *A Passage to India* only Godbole, who touches the eternal in mystical moments, perceives the transient link between it and our average experiences; and it is in the muddle of India, rather than in the chastened forms of Western art, that he attains a unity truly impervious to all disintegrating pressures.

The Wilcoxes are false to true English genius, as Forster defines it in a discussion of Chaucer's Canterbury pilgrims. The variety and vigor and good humor of Chaucer's people encouraged the clash of opinions that good temper then harmonized.[21] The present-day Wilcoxes, on the other hand, represent the inflexibly minded mercantile class and lack the imagination to reach the deepest aspects of truth. As Forster elsewhere expressed it in a 1920 article, humanity is only too prone to one-sidedness: habitually it puts off the moment of tolerance and the acknowledgment of our many-sidedness from today until tomorrow.[22]

It was Forster's aim to fuse into a single vision such opposed entities as body and soul, prose and poetry, fact and aspiration, intellect and mysticism. At times he attains in his fables the balance he seeks. At other times we might support Hynes, who finds that the novels illustrate the failure of the characters to connect rather than their reconciliation of the contrarieties of life. In any event, the novels are significant for the spirited efforts made by the central characters to achieve wholeness, whatever their success in such an enterprise may be.

IV   *The Natural World and Human Tradition*

One of Forster's links with nineteenth-century Romanticism is a belief in the fecundity of earth and in its regenerative powers. This earth philosophy is Wordsworthian; but, since Forster recognizes nature's sinister aspects, it is also Meredithian. Like George Meredith, Forster is often an aggressive pagan who finds in the external world the spirituality which the Christian religion centers in God. In *A Passage to India* Forster only tentatively asserts this trust in nature as leading to spiritual renewal, as in the concluding section when the autumn rains revive the parched earth. Still, Forster never abandoned the Romantic view of nature as a source of spiritual reality and moral inspiration, although India for much of the year is a wasteland inimical to life.

Forster has consistently been like the Voltaire whom he admires and whom he once characterized in *Abinger Harvest* as possessing an imagination "touched by the infinite variety of the natural world" (217). In his non-fiction Forster continued into the 1930's to romanticize nature as he had done earlier in *The Longest Journey* and in *Howards End*. Accordingly, he declared in 1931 that William Cowper bestows a gift which no one can covet or take from us—the English countryside in all its beauty and richness.[23] Forster cherishes the stability inherent in the rural tradition of which he feels a part; and he is as confident as he was in *Howards End* that the country resists being "claimed" or "standardized." [24] There is, granted, less effusiveness in these utterances than that which pervades, for example, the portrait of Stephen Wonham in *The Longest Journey* and less of the mystical transcendence symbolized by farm and elm in *Howards End*.

Increasingly nature has given Forster release from the intolerable aspects of modern life, even though he is less sure of such succor than he would have been in the nineteenth century when the stars were fixed and enshrined an ideal of majesty as well as a source of escape. They do still relieve us from the claims of human possessiveness and provide for us respite from the human world where our responsibilities, nevertheless, continue to lie.[25] Forster remains the partisan of the countryside and reiterates in *Goldsworthy Lowes Dickinson* (67) the hope he had expressed in *Howards End* that England may be on the verge of a "nature" mythology. In other essays he regrets the loss of our rural heritage with the growth of population, the spread of industrialism and scientific advances, and the inroads of the military. No wonder then that in *England's Pleasant Land* ([1940] 8) he celebrates this heritage and charts its decline, finding "a genuine and a tragic theme" in the development of the land over the centuries and in its present gradual destruction.

An aura of Romanticism likewise invests Forster's response to the past as it exerts its quickening influence. Memorials from the past sanctify the present since they suggest the continuity of the human spirit; the Cadbury Rings in *The Longest Journey*, for example, augment the perspective of that novel, and so in *Howards End* do the tumuli of the Danish soldiers, the Hertfordshire house, vine, and tree. In both books the most dynamic characters —Ansell, Rickie, Jackson, Stephen, Tony Failing in *The Longest Journey*; Ruth Wilcox, Ernst Schlegel, Schlegel's daughters in *Howards End*—find enlargement in the traditions of the race. The sensitive individual, whether he be a discriminating intellectual like the characters just mentioned or a devoted artist like the Alexandrian poet Cavafy, can draw warmth and power from the past. Cavafy, indeed, did find in it "something that transcended his local life and freshened and strengthened his art." [26]

In two key utterances Forster enunciates conflicting but actually complementary views on the historical past. In 1919 he wrote about it in a relaxed way in "Consolations of History," alleging that the satisfaction to be derived from it consists in fulfilled egotism and vanity. When we see the past spread before us, we are tempted to a display of dalliance, censure, pity, superiority, or Olympian knowledge that dramatizes our sense of vicarious power. In 1937 in "Recollectionism" Forster is more sober and more impersonal. The effect of memory, he maintains, is to infuse in us a sense of balance and perspective, often obscured by the actual event. From the discrete events of history, then, memory extracts a distillation, a quintessence, a spirit that has its immediate relevance. Life in the present can then be divested of its crudities and excrescences when the wisdom deriving from tradition throws them into relief.[27]

V *"The Mirror to Infinity": Personal Relationships*

Helen Schlegel in *Howards End* (1910) advances the view that personal relationships remain valid forever (28), and in "What I

Believe" (1938) Forster declares that they provide the only firm reality in a world of violence and cruelty. In a civilization which cherishes causes and abstractions, Forster asserts that the personal is the truly significant element. From our sustained relationships with others, we derive the most satisfying insight and wisdom that can come to us.

Since for Forster the sensibility is so significant, ultimate reality is psychological as well as mystical. In *Howards End* (81), depth of understanding between individuals presupposes, Forster says, a reality beyond them, a supernal presence that illuminates from the distance our activities as human beings in the foreground; only the private life "holds out the mirror to infinity." Twenty-five years later Forster similarly contended in *Goldsworthy Lowes Dickinson* (78) that human relationships, though they are not always ideal, do at their best convey a glimpse of the perfect. About the same time Forster wrote of Edward Carpenter's greatness and explained it in terms of this transcendent power of friendship:

. . . perhaps he never understood that for many people personal relationships are unimportant for the reason that their hearts are small. His own heart was great, and made him a great man. This is his secret so far as it can be put into words; the greatness of his heart, the depth of his humanity, the water that not only reflects the sky on its surface, but stretches down towards the centre of the globe, where all lines meet, and the many become the one.[28]

The civilization of the nineteenth century was in one respect preferable to our own, therefore, because men had more time for friendship and for "refining, expanding, correcting, and impairing personal relationships." [29]

Because the personal is so significant, isolation from other human beings means death to the spirit even if we enjoy prosperity. When communications snap between people, "the human race freezes to death in the dark." So Forster says in an introduction to Donald Windham's *The Warm Country* (1962), but he might also have been describing the tragic aspects of *Howards End*: the actual and potential stagnation of the Wilcoxes, the alienation of Leonard Bast, and the anguish of Margaret Schlegel at the division which has come between herself and her sister. The theme of separation from others, of course, dominates in *A Passage to India* where good intentions and the humanistic virtues can no longer quite span the void between individuals and the races. Only with the energies let loose by the Hindu festival can these divisions be overcome and a satisfying spiritual communion be intimated, a communion in which the purely personal is reinforced by—or lost in—the cosmic forces which surround the characters.

Forster indicts the British public for its sexual hypocrisy and for its subservience to convention, tendencies which negate the personal element. For Henry Wilcox in *Howards End* there is something unwholesome about sex, and he cannot enjoy passion because he cannot accept it frankly. And Forster tells us in *Marianne Thornton* (210) how unbearable Henry Thornton's life became when he went contrary to Victorian law and married his deceased wife's sister: "To the amoralist it will offer yet another example of the cruelty and stupidity of the English law in matters of sex," law promulgated and sustained by people like the Wilcoxes in *Howards End*. Forster maintains, in short, as in "My Wood" of *Abinger Harvest*, that we need not deny or suppress our "materialism" and our "carnality" but that we must purposively direct them.

Forster upon occasion regards passion as subsidiary to companionship. In *The Longest Journey*, Rickie's friendship with Ansell rescues him from the destroying influence of his wife, Agnes. Sexual passion itself may pass over into an asexual relationship. In *Howards End*, Margaret Schlegel is impelled by passion to marry Henry Wilcox, whose standards are mostly at variance with her own. She regards her decision as a right one, and she is willing to suspend intellectual independence in order to know the exaltation of love. But the house and tree at Howards End imply that, for a permanent relationship, comradeship is superior to sex. So Forster approaches in the end, perhaps, the asceticism he had denied in the beginning.

Love can reach beyond sex to include the whole of mankind; and Eros can become Agapé to the degree that it aligns us with our fellow men. Like Dickinson, we can embrace the cardinal values of Christianity and believe that "we are members one with another" (114). The uncorrupted Rickie Elliot of *The Longest Journey*—admirable for his kindness, consideration, and generosity—and such agnostics as Margaret Schlegel and Cyril Fielding actually do embrace the virtues implicit in a "liberal" Christianity. As Forster declared in *Alexandria* (84), the chief strength of Christian Alexandria was its clinging to the notion of love, to the concept "that the best thing on earth is likely to be the best in heaven." Perhaps he most aptly summarized this aspect of his thought when he viewed himself in 1944 as "a sentimentalist who believes in the importance of love" and when he declared that the desire to love and to be loved keeps the race human.[30]

In the early days of World War II, Forster was, however, suspicious of love as a civilizing agent. The greatest of all forces in private life, he feared, might mislead in public affairs and provide a less certain means for social reconstruction than would tolerance. In "The Unsung Virtue of Tolerance" (1953), he brought tolerance and love closer together by maintaining that love is "the heavenly counterpart" of tolerance.[31] Love is positive in its inception and operation; tolerance, negative. Love provides, says Forster, a satisfying explanation of our earthly existence; but tolerance may avert disaster from it. Love and tolerance are both opposed to passivity and complacency: tolerance risks the loss of political advantage and may entail various embarrassments; love risks destruction by one's personal enemies.[32]

VI "The Glories and the Dangers of Independence": The Individual versus the Community

The individual in Forster's view has worth, not only socially and politically, but metaphysically as he achieves, progressively, a state of inner illumination. In a critique of Ibsen, Forster explores the difficult relationship existing between authority and freedom: assert individuality, and we may give rise to war and chaos; suppress it, and we may have no life.[33] Clearly, the evils following upon suppression are greater than those following upon moral anarchy. Whereas the aggrandizement of the ego may have its dangers, we can guard against them if we know them for what they are. Egoism can face two ways: without imagination, it becomes the "vilest" aspect of life; with imagination, the "highest." [34]

Forster, accordingly, admires a writer like Gide who remained an individual in an age which encouraged conformity; or, in *Two Cheers for Democracy*, one like Forrest Reid who existed in his own right as a person, totally unlike anyone else whom Forster ever knew (229, 269). As we view the great men from the past, we perceive that only a certain kind of individual transcends time and mere considerations of chronology: the man described in "Consolations of History" whose development is manifold, whose

self-sufficiency becomes moral vision, and whose pursuit of consecrated aims is intense. As Forster explained in *Alexandria* (32)
and in *Two Cheers for Democracy* (9–11), only by recognizing
"the glories and the dangers of independence" can the individual
discover himself, attain the preeminence that is his right, and
leave behind all pressures that would bind and oppress.

In the conflict of the individual with the community, Forster
favors the individual. For there is something to be said for "the
unadvertised, the unorganized, the unscheduled" life represented
by the poet Cowper which our materialistic and standardized society would subvert.[35] Although the community must have its due,
the individual also has his rights and privileges. Forster would
thus challenge Christopher Caudwell's view that men can only
achieve liberty through their actions in society. Communists are,
in fact, individuals, and thus emphasize, Forster observes, the cat-
egory which they also challenge. We must be more skeptical than
Caudwell was of "the long view." [36] We must rather seek understanding in the here and now of the individual's aspirations as
opposed to the simplifications of social theory.

The liberal orders his sensitivity, his intellect, and his powers of
contemplative insight to encourage from within a change of heart
in himself and others. Perhaps this purposeful cultivation of the
private self, of good will and charity, is basic to meaningful social
action, especially since, as Forster said, so many of the panaceas
of the 1930's were not radical enough. Rearmament, limited rearmament, and communism were partial, sometimes misguided,
modes in the 1930's for saving civilization. The only sure basis for
reform, Forster maintained, lies in the appeal to the individual's
conscience and to his sense of identification with other men as
components of the human race.[37]

Such a view, Christian in its desire for brotherhood, underlies
Howards End and *A Passage to India*. Leonard Bast can only be
helped, Margaret Schlegel insists, by an opportunity to develop
self-respect; and he can't be helped at all so long as people ab-
stractly deem him a worker, as the Wilcoxes do, or a social case, as
the Schlegels do. With respect to *A Passage to India*, the excesses
of the Anglo-Indians can only be counteracted by kindness and by
something going beyond kindness, an "occasional intoxication of
the blood." In a 1946 article, "India Again" (*Two Cheers*), Forster similarly contends that good will is not enough, and that Indi-

ans and Europeans must cultivate affection, rooted in a common human need, to enhance their understanding of each other.

The conscientious liberal must also turn outward to the world, as Forster has assiduously done. Contrary to the notion encouraged by such critics as Savage and Cox, even by Trilling, Forster has not been uncommitted. Disregard of the uncollected miscellaneous prose has led to the conception of Forster as a withdrawn, disengaged thinker, writer, and man of letters. He is, of course, aware of the claims of private life; but these claims do not negate, in his view, the intellectual's public responsibilities.[38] The artist does, however, present a special case because he must not let his social and political views determine the content of his writing: he should postpone his commitment, as Forster once said, until the last moment.[39]

But on basic matters the artist and the intellectual must on occasion declare themselves even if they make the public uncomfortable by their nonconformity.[40] Thus Forster has firmly voiced his own ideas in the last thirty years. Far from being the work of a disengaged intellectual, the essays in *Two Cheers for Democracy* are, as Forster truly said, "political" in their climate. In certain circumstances commitment is imperative for the humanist, just as in others aloofness leads to the surest perceptions. Both Matthew Arnold and Goldsworthy Lowes Dickinson, Forster maintains, realized the humanist's complex role as he must decide between the demands of the self to be left in isolation and those of society upon the self.

Two uncollected items, a "Notes on the Way" (*Time and Tide*, November 2, 1935) and "The Ivory Tower" [41] illuminate this subject. In pursuit of the private life, a radiance and a poise, impossible to acquire in active life, result; but pangs of conscience and the need to assume responsibility may also assert themselves. Nevertheless, when we enter the arena, our balance and perspective are likely to be upset by the pressures operating there. In "The Ivory Tower" Forster asserts that both the passive and the active modes of life are needed for civilization; the individual must satisfy both his instinct for "solitude" and his instinct for "multitude." The withdrawn life encourages mysticism, abstract thought, and the detailed contemplation of events. Such detachment, Forster claims, is as indispensable for the public official to acquire as the tangible civic virtues. Our duty, in short, is to save both ourselves and the community. As V. S. Pritchett has maintained, Forster's distinction has been his carrying the private voice into the public place, his insistence that personal values have greater relevance in resolving social and political issues than the Edwardian bourgeoisie had assumed.

The accommodating of the two ways of life to one another is also the theme of "The Challenge of Our Time" (*Two Cheers*). Our present-day challenge, says Forster, is to combine the best in the personal and the civic spheres: "the Old Morality," with its emphasis on liberty and individuality, and "the New Economy," with its sense of social justice and responsibility. As one who is in part a Victorian liberal, he is interested still in laissez-faire, but laissez-faire in the realm of the spirit only. Social planning will be necessary for our physical welfare, but planning should stop with the body's requirements; the mind and spirit must have complete liberty.

Early in his career Forster evinced the liberalism that was with the years to grow more impassioned and public. He contributed essays and reviews to the *Independent Review,* a periodical founded by Dickinson and others in 1903 to enable conscientious Cambridge intellectuals to express their dissatisfaction with a complacent society.[42] Forster's own contributions were not political, but he found the magazine and its staff congenial. The fact that he contributed to the review indicates, as Frederick C. Crews has remarked in *E.M. Forster: The Perils of Humanism* (31), that Forster must have endorsed "its repeated emphasis on freedom of discussion, equality of opportunity, and the importance of the individual man."

From 1919 to 1921, Forster, as the literary editor of the *Daily Herald,* was in apparent agreement with the socialism advocated by the newspaper; and then and later he contributed to liberal periodicals. Like others of his generation he was involved in World War I (he served in Egypt with the Red Cross, 1915–19) and was later disillusioned with it. In the war years and in the 1920's he became interested in questions of imperial policy, especially after his second visit to India (1921). In his writings on Egypt and India, he advocated a policy at once more imaginative and more cognizant of realities than that of England seemed to him to be.[43] On this subject, of course, he expressed himself most persuasively in *A Passage to India.*

During the 1930's Forster compensated, perhaps consciously, for his inability to create fiction by much miscellaneous writing. Although he was concerned with literature, he was even more absorbed by public questions. He protested against restrictions imposed by the government on the freedom of expression of writers and intellectuals;[44] he desired social justice for the many, especially an economic independence for them compatible with the precedents of English freedom;[45] and he reacted sharply to infringements placed upon the individual's liberty. On the one hand, he deplored such developments as the "Fabio-Fascism" or bureaucracy that had begun to determine all aspects of British life; on the other hand, he deplored such specific curtailment of prerogatives as those contained in the Incitement to Disaffection Bill.[46]

As an active member and as president of the National Council for Civil Liberties, Forster did much to heighten opposition to this and other restrictive statutes. He detected, moreover, the dangers to liberty in the activities of one like Mosley who challenged the government but did so in an irresponsible and authoritarian way.[47] If shadows of injustice overlaid British liberty in the 1930's, the benefits deriving from such liberty outweighed in Forster's mind the inequalities still existing at home and in the empire abroad;[48] and he increasingly became the spokesman for those who espoused the democratic freedoms. During the early 1930's he was pacifist in his public utterances, regarding war as the ultimate imbecility; and he vigorously supported the League of Nations.[49]

Toward the end of the decade Forster followed the pattern of many other intellectuals and modified his pacifism when the Nazi oppressions became more open. He touched upon many aspects of the international menace. In "Post Munich" (1939), he advocated stoic endurance in a time of crisis; in "They Hold Their Tongues" (1939), he regretted the prohibitions placed in wartime upon the civilized minority; and in "Three Anti-Nazi Broadcasts" (1940), he expressed his absolute revulsion from the theories and practices of the German leaders. In particular, he was revolted by the emphasis upon Nordic supremacy and the suppression of the Jewish peoples.[50]

He was also critical of communism, but to a lesser degree in the 1930's than he was of nazism. He recognized the idealism of many Communist converts, and he was sympathetic to their desire for social revolution; but he distrusted from the beginning the authoritarian aspect of Russian communism.[51] After World War II he continued to be vocal about social and political issues, as his letters to the press (many of them jointly signed) indicate. He has recently declared himself on such subjects as the British Broadcasting Company's third program, Hungarian authors, the Wolfenden Report on homosexuality, the suspension of nuclear weapons tests, the apartheid policy of South Africa, capital punishment, and the Chinese invasion of India.[52] If we view his career since the publication of *A Passage to India* in 1924, it is difficult, then, to challenge a *Times* editorial for January 1, 1958: "No sensible liberal cause has lacked his backing; no obvious excess in the public life of the past thirty years but has earned his censure; and no one, in private, has done more to deserve the laurels he has heaped on him in public."

Underlying his political attitudes there have been consistent values which Forster often defended and acted upon. He is a democrat insofar as he supports the individualism encouraged by free institutions. Democracy allows liberty and criticism, and it is therefore worth two cheers; when it encourages distinction, it may be worth three (*Two Cheers*, 69–70). Forster recognizes the paradoxes of British democracy: "muddling, protesting, heroic, whining, materialistic, wanting food, wanting peace, wanting war, braving death." Unifying these inconsistencies, however, there is the upward urge to achieve "pure Liberty," to reach "to the Beloved Republic which feeds upon Freedom and lives, to the Good Place which is every poet's dream." [53] In a democracy two processes operate, according to Forster in his remarks upon Orwell. There is the negative process of reaching patriotism, wherein, if we cannot find salvation, we can at least "prefer the less bad to the more bad, and so become patriots, while keeping our brains and hearts intact." There is the more positive faith in liberty, the possibility of finding more of it in England than in Stalin's Russia or Franco's Spain, and the realization that we need more rather than less freedom (*Two Cheers*, 62–63).

Conventions are valid to the degree that one apprehends them imaginatively and uses them generously in pursuing the personal and the moral life. Forster's conscientious humanists like Rickie Elliot, Margaret Schlegel, and Cyril Fielding protest against the forms which harden social existence, not against the forms which enrich it. Even Samuel Butler, the arch-iconoclast, was an advocate of firmly conceived standards, so long as their implications were "humane" (*Two Cheers*, 221). If Forster's own ancestors, the Thorntons, displayed an upper-middle-class self-complacency, they also had redeeming virtues, traditional as much as personal in origin: "affections, comfort, piety, integrity, intelligence, public activity, private benevolence," and a confident belief in a future life (*Marianne Thornton*, 20). In their attitudes the Thorntons were somewhere between the unimaginative, materialistic Wilcoxes and the compassionate, idealistic Schlegels of *Howards End*.

Forster could criticize the aristocracy and the upper middle class for confusing the right to privileges with class origin and the prerogatives of a gentleman with social justice and political rectitude, but he also perceived the positive features of social traditions. In "The P.E.N. and the Sword" (1947), he remarks that during his stay in Lithuania, he found that warm-heartedness, hospitality, and a sense of the soil were compensations for the shallowness, the effete feudalism, and the occasional arrogance of an "unprogressive society." [54] He is in sympathy with aristocratic values when they determine character but skeptical of them when they lead to social exclusiveness.

And in his awareness of middle-class complacency, he celebrates the virtues of the extreme classes: the aristocracy and the populace. These classes at their best have a vigor, an independence, and a gaiety lacking in the middle class. Although an aristocratic order is not always just or permanent, the loss of its influence means that something forthright is passing from social life ("Mrs. Miniver," *Two Cheers*). The enfeebling tradition or the repressive convention, however, always brought Forster to the attack. In such protests he condemned prescriptive thinking, excessive propriety and hypocrisy, and the rationalization of questionable standards by an irrelevant appeal to spiritual, moral, and religious absolutes.

VII "*This Contradictory and Disquieting World*"

Ultimately, the essence of life eludes definition; and its circumstances are often unpredictable. Since it is in some degree haphazard and chaotic, it cannot devolve in purely ordered patterns. In Forster's world, as Hyatt H. Waggoner says,[55] men do not know enough to control natural, let alone moral, evil, even if, as we

have seen, Forster conceives the humanist's responsibility to be
that of utilizing reason to secure the greatest degree of internal
and external order. In Forster's world, as in Hardy's, coincidence
predominates; and sudden, seemingly unmotivated deaths are
more frequent than they are in actual life. Yet these deaths, Waggoner alleges, symbolize the intrusion of the unpredictable into
our regulated existences. The coincidences, he says, also illustrate
a contrary truth: the density of the web which connects the apparently unrelated phenomena and incidents of life. Another of
Forster's interpreters, Frederick C. Crews (165), expresses a similar view: the ironies and sudden deaths establish "an atmosphere
of instability" and induce our distrust of "specious certainties."

Despite Forster's intermittent distrust of modern psychology,
he has long been aware of the importance of the unconscious for
esthetic creativity. In "English Prose between 1918 and 1939," collected in *Two Cheers for Democracy,* he asserts that the artist's
recourse to the irrational has given a complication and richness to
portrayals of human nature in recent literature (274). In "What I
Believe" (in the same collection), he acknowledges that modern
psychology has shattered the idea of a "person" who is statically
integrated in his powers, and has proved that eruptive violences
exist in the psyche (68). Even before Freud became popular,
Forster had been aware of the latent irrationalities of human nature: Gino's murderous hysteria when he learns of the death of his
child in *Where Angels Fear to Tread,* the Dionysian exuberance of
Stephen Wonham in *The Longest Journey,* and the casual street
murder of one Florentine by another in *A Room with a View.*

Life is not only irrational and unpredictable, but it resists our
attempts to define it with precision. It is replete with ambiguities,
the ramifications of which are difficult to trace with sureness. In
fact, one measure of an individual's insight and understanding is
just this knowledge (such as Desmond MacCarthy possessed [56])
of the contradictions underlying the simplest statements. In com-
menting on William Golding's terrifying vision in *Lord of the
Flies,* Forster sees it as facing two ways, toward horror and toward beauty.[57] A. E. Housman was another writer whose work
illustrates the major incongruities underlying experience even if
he did not always recognize them or satisfactorily resolve them:
he denied God at the same time that he denounced Him; he
praised both virtue and license; he cherished the phantasmal

while he denied the force of illusion; he was convinced of treachery everywhere while he dreamed of affection; his manner is "scholarly and churchified," while his matter is "blood-hot or death-cold." [58]

Those writers, according to Forster, are the wisest who acknowledge the strength of such contrary impulsions. Thus George Orwell followed the implications of his experience whether they took him into the "unseen" or around the corner. He wished to learn, in any event, as much as possible of "this contradictory and disquieting world" (*Two Cheers*, 63). And Gide was always aware of the involutions and convolutions of the moral life, "the delight, the difficulty, the duty of registering that complexity and of conveying it" (232).

Forster is skeptical of science and its results, especially when the intelligence acts oblivious of ethical considerations. Yet his own intelligence allowed Forster to supplement the idealism of his humanistic philosophy with more rigorous concepts. His is no blind faith in human possibilities, no unconsidered belief in the nobility of man's nature and the rightness of all his impulses. Balancing Forster's Romantic enthusiasms, there is his consciousness of man's limitations. If he protested in 1955 against those modern thinkers who emphasize original sin and thereby undermine the humanistic view of life, he is in sympathy in 1962 with the somber view of human nature dramatized by William Golding in *Lord of the Flies*.[59] In that novel, Piggy, the repository of intelligence, is defeated; but he is nevertheless to be admired for his estimate of the forces raised against him and for his efforts to live by the light of his mind.

Golding presents in parable form, Forster observes, the fall of man who, under certain circumstances, relapses from rationality to bestiality. Forster seemingly now acknowledges that darkness, as well as light, dwells in man's soul and that man is predisposed toward evil as well as good. Forster knew before World War II, moreover, that it was possible to sin, as Lady Macbeth did, "through the depths of her own soul." Like many other human beings, she did not need to encounter the witches to know evil and to have it regulate her actions.[60] The possibilities of such degradation arising from within man's own nature, not the threat from without of alien ideologies, became for Forster in the 1930's the primary menace to civilization. Forster also appreciated in *As-*

pects of the Novel the truth of Melville's dramatization of evil in *Moby Dick* and *Billy Budd* (140–43) and how he was compelled to introduce the concept of original sin to right the metaphysical balance of the world he knew.

Forster's consciousness of the presence of evil forces in human nature and in society informs the confessional "What I Believe." This essay is less optimistic in tenor than some of the earlier prose pieces, but also less pessimistic than *A Passage to India*. Tolerance, good temper, sympathy—the humanistic virtues—are all precious attributes; but unfortunately, says Forster, they are not widely effective in a world characterized by religious and racial persecution, in which ignorance rules and in which science has been deflected from altruistic ends. Still, in a world of violence, personal relationships, if they are not powerful, provide evidence that values other than empirically perceived ones exist and that men have noble impulses as well as insidious instincts. We can believe still in the residual goodness of human nature; we can, with respect to human possibilities, still "shelter a flickering flame." [61] Forster concludes that earthly life is not a failure but a tragedy, principally because it is difficult to translate private decencies into public ones.

In more recent utterances, Forster has voiced this qualified pessimism. Writing to K. Natwar-Singh, Forster has expressed a quiet desperation, if not a complete despair:

The world is in a strange state and we all need each other's greetings. . . . I expect that a few islets in Cambridge and elsewhere will remain uncovered for longer than I shall, so I don't worry personally, which is in all circumstances a mistake. Still, when I reflect what the human race might do and feel, and observe what people do do and how they don't feel, I naturally get depressed.

Forster expresses himself in similar tone to the same correspondent as he says: "When I try to conjecture the immediate future of this energetic planet, I am divided between interest and gloom. All the values I appreciate are disappearing and I don't want to outlive them. . . ." [62]

And yet the humanism which he represents has weathered the attacks leveled against it, Forster thinks. Such at least is the gist of a letter Forster wrote in 1951, discussing Melville and his own recent activity as a librettist for Benjamin Britten's *Billy Budd*.

Forster cites the remarks of William Plomer on Melville's poetry. Plomer had recognized that Melville believed in fate but was not completely fatalistic. Forster is in apparent agreement with Melville's position as Plomer describes it:

He believed in fate not free-will; maintained skepticism; and honoured simple people, sensual pleasures and works of art—wisdom hammered or visions won from joy or suffering. He did not look to a rosy future for mankind: ignorance and unreason, war and greed were bound to postpone if not to prevent that. On the other hand, he did not sink into misanthropy, for he had experience or perceptions of as "much as man might hope and more than heaven may mean." [68]

Plomer's remarks, in Forster's view, present a reasoned balance between the pessimistic and optimistic impulses. Plomer's essay on Melville's poetry, Forster asserts, "centers on the central warmth and on the bonfire in the heart and on the Milk of Paradise. Possessed of these, we can flourish and endure and understand. Not all is lost. All cannot be lost. The hero hangs dead from the yard arm, dead irredeemably and not in any heaven, dead as a doornail, dead as Antigone, and he has given us life." Such is the chastened, deeply felt, and tragic humanism that underlies Forster's work as philosopher and creative artist. Such seems to be his current view on the meaning of experience to human beings.

CHAPTER 2

The Italian Novels and the Short Stories

I *"Midway in Our Life's Journey"*: Where Angels
Fear to Tread

*W*HERE Angels Fear to Tread has attained wide esteem
and becomes more incisive on each reading. Frank Swinnerton in *The Georgian Scene* (393) has judged it to be, in consistency of tone and invention, the best of Forster's books; and F.
R. Leavis in "E.M. Forster" (262) thinks it "the most successful of
the prewar novels." Even a critic like Crews (71), who feels that
The Longest Journey and *Howards End* are more complex and
sophisticated, finds that Forster exerts in it extraordinary control;
and he emphasizes its formal excellence. For a short book, the
scope of *Where Angels Fear to Tread* is broad; it presents a contrast in national types, an analysis of various temperaments comprising the English middle class, a comedy of manners exposing
the hypocrisies of this class, a romance in which forces of good
oppose those of evil, and a tragedy originating in the substitution
of convention for charity and imagination.

The novel divides into two main sections, each focusing on a
journey which Philip Herriton undertakes, as spokesman for his
suburban Sawston family, to Italy. The first time he goes he hopes
to prevent his widowed sister-in-law Lilia from marrying Gino
Carella, a dentist's son in the mountain village of Monteriano. He
arrives too late, only to be toppled onto a bed by Gino for his
pains. Lilia's friend, Caroline Abbott, had helped arrange the
marriage; and she eventually becomes the heroine as she travels
from Sawston's bourgeois values to a more open life in Italy. As
for the shallow Lilia, Gino humiliates her and is unfaithful; and
somewhat later she escapes an intolerable life by dying in childbirth.

On his second journey to Italy, Philip wishes to negotiate with
Gino about adopting the baby boy. Caroline Abbott is also in
Italy for the same purpose: she hopes to atone for her part in
Lilia's marriage by devoting herself to the child. Both Philip and

Caroline give over their plans, however, when they realize the depth of Gino's paternal passion. They overlook the evil genius of Philip's sister Harriet, who kidnaps the baby without Philip's sanction. The carriage in which the Herritons leave Monteriano for the station in the valley overturns in a rainstorm; the baby is killed and Philip's arm broken. When he brings news of the disaster to Gino, Gino tortures him by alternately twisting his arm and suffocating him. Caroline comes upon them in time to save Philip, and she manages, with her goddess-like dignity, to reconcile the men. Although she has by this time succumbed to Gino's charm, she is unable to reveal her love to him. Philip's own dawning love for Caroline is deflected when on the way home from Italy she confesses her unrequited passion for Gino. If Philip and Caroline are both unfulfilled, they have at least become aware, through the liberating influence of Italy, of possibilities heretofore unknown to them.

The idea of the life-pilgrimage is central in the book. The opening lines from Dante's *The Divine Comedy,* which Gino quotes in the second chapter of the novel, inform us that in "the middle of life's journey" the poet has felt most deeply the weight of his destiny and has experienced the revelation which gives him peace. The two central characters—Philip and Caroline—are also some distance along in their lives when the novel opens; they undergo profound disturbances as the novel progresses; and they eventually return—but greatly altered—to the "true way" that they had lost or had never fully known.

It was no accident that, until his publishers intervened, Forster intended to name his book "Monteriano," [1] for it is in what Italy signifies to his characters that Forster found his structural principle. Italy is the background presence to which all else is referred, and the characters are valued as they relate to that country. On the second trip to Italy Philip arrives at the truth of what Italy means. He and Caroline Abbott have just been "converted" to the South by sharing enthusiasm for *Lucia di Lammermoor.* At this point Philip is looking at the Piazza of Monteriano and suddenly comprehends the unity which Monteriano, as a microcosm of all Italy, embodies; "the Palazzo Pubblico, the Collegiate Church, and the Caffè Garibaldi: the intellect, the soul, and the body" (146).

Philip follows a vacillating course toward enlightenment, as the force exerted by Italy either fails to affect him or stirs him deeply. On his earlier travels his confrontation of Italy had been esthetic rather than moral; he has yet to learn "that human love and love of truth sometimes conquer where love of beauty fails" (69). He has been unable to remold or to reject Sawston; with the failure of his prophetic estheticism, he has taken refuge in sardonic humor toward Sawston and her people. His fascination with Italy and his negative appraisal of Sawston last until Lilia decides to marry Gino. His revulsion from Gino demonstrates that his understanding had been superficial and that his unconventionality had been shallow. Yet Philip's total progress is to be measured in terms of his appreciation of the open, spontaneous, and life-infusing values of primitive Italy and of his distaste for the proprieties and hypocrisies of the English middle class.

As soon as Philip reaches Italy on his second journey, the spell of the South begins to work. Although he regards the railroad station at Florence as the center of "beastly Italy," he even now feels that "enchantment" lurks just beneath the surface of his discomfiting experiences. When he gets to Monteriano, he succumbs reluctantly to its charm as his sister Harriet decisively isolates herself from it. He is aware, however, that Italy can still expose him to ridicule when, for instance, he makes a child guide unhappy by overpaying her. But, when Caroline conveys to him Gino's regrets for his former rudeness, he feels that things have again come right, that Italy has indeed become "beautiful, courteous, lovable, as of old" (111).

If Philip now knows that Monteriano embodies truths that Sawston never suspects, he is not yet prepared to act upon his knowledge. As Caroline Abbott divines and as he admits, life for him is a spectacle with transfiguring moments. She condemns his indecisiveness but admires his wisdom and understanding. She herself has been reoriented in Italy and becomes an oracle who gives Philip knowledge of himself. After their conversation in the church at Santa Deodata, the center of Monteriano's spiritual life, Philip not only admits that she was right about his irresolution but he also begins to love her, even though in Sawston he had thought of her as an uninteresting and unattractive woman.

Critics have generally identified Philip with Monteriano's Santa Deodata.[2] Just as Philip in his earliest phase was an esthete in his ivory tower, the saint was remote from active life. Philip gazes at the saint's figure in the Collegiate Church frescoes when he talks to Caroline; at this point, Forster asserts that neither in life nor in death did the saint accomplish much and implies that Philip's life up to this time has also been purposeless. Yet Philip in his regenerate phase leaves such passivity behind. He gives over trying to secure the baby (he does not realize until too late that Harriet has kidnapped it), and he acts decisively in confessing the baby's death to Gino. The saint, however, has a quixotic intensity strong enough to capture the hearts of the town's inhabitants, a quality that Philip possesses only slightly. While Santa Deodata's humorless religion has also some affinities with Harriet's "back kitchen" evangelicism, Santa Deodata herself has a depth of feeling which is Latinate and "religious" and which to some extent excuses her selfishness, just as a similar intensity compensates in part for Gino's brutality.

At this time of reconciliation with Italy, Philip again overestimates her glamour and forgets that sordidness, violence, and primitive passion are realities as true now of Italian life as they have ever been. After he relates the death of the baby to Gino, Philip is unprepared for a brutality that is as much Gino's birthright as is his geniality.

Throughout his second sojourn in Italy Philip extends his knowledge of life. He realizes, for example, that all have contributed to the death of Gino's child. Even Gino, we can infer, set in motion the wheels of his own destruction by sending the taunting postcards to the baby's half-sister in England, thereby antagonizing the Herritons. Nor has Caroline in her benevolence been selfless. Yet Philip feels that only he has been trivial and cowardly, and he realizes that his own role in the senseless tragedy has been crucial. In his enlightenment, he now sees that Italy combines all facets of experience into a dynamic synthesis. She does not evade the violent, the evil, and the sinister; but, in confronting them honestly, she negates their influence in favor of the good, the beautiful, and the true.

Closer contact with Caroline makes Philip's transformation complete. He can now believe that greatness is possible, as he regards her prophetic countenance: "Her eyes were open, full of infinite pity and full of majesty, as if they discerned the boundaries of sorrow, and saw unimaginable tracts beyond. Such eyes he had seen in great pictures but never in a mortal" (173). She has been transformed from a timid rebel to a woman who sees beyond good and evil to the region of the eternal verities. Her outward mien goes from that of an unimpressive woman to that of a goddess who commands others by what she is. In the baby-bathing sequence, she achieves beauty and serenity, this time not of a pagan goddess but of the Virgin Mary. When Caroline intervenes to save Philip from Gino, she becomes a Pallas Athena figure presiding ritually over the reconciliation of the men by insisting that they drink the milk the maid has prepared for the dead baby. Existence in England may once more be humdrum for Philip, but he now sees life critically and in its full integrity. Sawston will never claim his undivided loyalty, nor will it claim Caroline's. Imagination has ennobled both of them.

Caroline Abbott undergoes vacillations similar to Philip's, although she has more self-possession. Possibly because of her uncertainties, she becomes, as one critic has said, the most "surprising" and "touching" of Forster's "guardian" figures[3]—people whose intuitive wisdom guides others. Before the trip with Lilia, Caroline had impressed Philip as grave, nice-looking, decorous, charming, and sober but not much else, respectable rather than vital. Yet she had had a moment of liberation in Italy when she encouraged Lilia, in revolt against Sawston, to marry Gino. She had awakened on this first visit to "beauty and splendor," so much so that she alone, of all the women he had ever known, had seemed to Gino to be "simpatico." This is a tacit admission that he and Caroline have affinities which might, under more favorable circumstances, have reached fruition in the sexual bond. But Italy's challenge to Caroline's sensibilities on her first visit has not been deep enough to change her basically.

On her second trip to Italy, Caroline reveals at first a single-minded intention to get control of Gino's child; she agrees with Harriet that Gino has no sense of sin and that he "murdered" Lilia. While she talks in this vein to Philip, she strokes the outlines of a Gothic window and, in so doing, becomes physically identified with one of Monteriano's manifestations of the spirit, its architecture. An inner liberation begins as her humane instincts assert themselves and take her further than her conscious ideas would sanction. The Italy of tradition has begun its mellowing effect on her, as upon Philip; for it is by this window, as they look at the towers opposite, that they achieve their first understanding.

She turns from such exalted emotion to a recognition of her purpose at Monteriano: "to champion morality and purity, and the holy life of an English home" (124). But in her dreams that night, music and beauty and laughter penetrate to unsettle her; and Poggibonsi, the town traditionally antagonistic to Monteriano, becomes for her, like Sawston, "a joyless, straggling place, full of people who pretended" (125). She can no longer deny the power of Italy's bustling energies which swept over her at the opera earlier that evening.

Both Philip and Caroline are educated to the complexities of life and are no longer content with the simplifications of experience which satisfy the inhabitants of Sawston. Even before his first mission, Philip had been disillusioned with the Italy of romance and with Lilia for marrying a dentist's son. A painful éclaircissement followed because false romance "which cannot resist the unexpected and the incongruous and the grotesque" (27) departed forever from him. For Italy teaches him that melodrama is possible, that experience can be lurid, exaggerated, and unpredictable.

Such is the drift of the concluding incidents. At this point the idiot messenger sent by Harriet to Philip represents perfectly the departures from the norm so characteristic of pagan Italy: "In another country he would have been shut up; here he was accepted as a public institution, and part of Nature's scheme" (158). The idiot is a ghastly creature, but he too has his distinction: he has visions of the saints, visions not accorded everyone. Even such a creature is assimilated to the moral drama, being aligned by his vitality with the forces of good as they confront and rout those of evil.

The towers which dominate the skyline of Monteriano dominate the spiritual landscape of the novel. Many of the towers are broken (only seventeen of the original fifty-two remain), signifying that modern Italy may lack the full integration of powers that characterized her during the Middle Ages and the Renaissance. In comparison to modern England, Italy still retains a sense of the complexities of experience; and the towers emphasize this truth. They look skyward but have their feet in the earth. They connote aspiration in their upward reaches; they convey mundane experience at their bases (they are often placarded with advertisements); and they reach in their foundations toward the nether regions. If, as Philip says, the tower opposite "reaches up to heaven and down to the other place," and is thereby "a symbol of the town" (113), tower and town both signify the elusive complications of Italy and, by extension, of human life itself.

The scene of much violence in the past, the towers represent, as James McConkey maintains in *The Novels of E.M. Forster* (102), both "an admirable simplicity of elemental passion" and a "darkness and confused violence." They also symbolize to Lilia in their moonlit beauty a freedom that is denied her in the frustrating marriage to Gino. In Philip's first view of them, they are lit by the rays of the declining sun and become emblems of Italy's magical beauty. They contribute, moreover, to the insubstantial aspect of Monteriano viewed from a distance, the towers then becoming as masts for "some fantastic ship city of a dream" (27).

The other characters in the novel do not develop, possibly because they do not respond to the influence of Italy. One of them, Harriet, is described as "the same in Italy as in England—changing her disposition never, and her atmosphere under protest" (114). This uniformity, in varying manifestations, can also be found in Lilia, Gino, and Mrs. Herriton. These characters impress us by what they are rather than what they become. Like Harriet, who is "acrid, indissoluble, large," they impress as commanding presences rather than as subtly envisioned personalities. With the exception of the weak Lilia, there is something monolithic about these characters in the singleness of their energies and in the concentration of their purposes. They attain a stature convincing in its own terms, the strength that is to be associated with caricature (Harriet and Mrs. Herriton), or with an easygoing normality (Gino and Lilia), or with a primal vital force (Gino).

Gino is complex to the degree that the Italy he represents is a nation whose qualities are not easily defined. He is complex rather than subtle, and his attributes have been fixed by his environment. No more than Lilia or Harriet is he capable of self-criticism and of intelligent analysis of his own motives. Gino's excessive concern with the proprieties even provides an unexpected link with Sawston, different as he is from the English middle class in most other respects. He is content enough to exploit the double-standard of sexual morality; and he lacks any consciousness of the incongruities of his own actions. He cannot realize that his situation is national as well as personal, "that generations of ancestors, good, bad, or indifferent, forbad the Latin man to be chivalrous to the northern woman, the northern woman to forgive the Latin man" (65).

Gino's life is led at the instinctive rather than the intellectual level, despite his familiarity with Dante. Accordingly, he is both violent and magnanimous, vindictive and open-hearted. There is, at points, a hint of the demonic about him. His silent and explosive laughter when Philip accosts him; his stalking of Lilia like an enraged animal when she threatens to cut off her money from him; and the fiendishness of his anger and revenge at the end of the novel are instances of his uncontrolled passion. To the intruding Caroline Abbott, Gino's smoke rings seem as if a breath from the pit.

But this hint of the demonic is also an indication of the depths of life to be found in him. For he thinks not only in terms of gratifying his animal impulses but of their relationship to the larger history of the race: he sees his son as the only sure guarantee of his own immortality and Italy's. He has his unexpected generosities also. He not only forgives Philip but perjures himself for Philip's benefit at the inquest over the baby's death. He has sure intuitions where his affections are involved, and he penetrates the very depths of his friend's nature: in the future, "he would pull out Philip's life, turn it inside out, remodel it, and advise him how to use it for the best" (174). As a real person, Gino is somewhat less convincing than the other characters because he is less extensively analyzed and shown less often in action. But he is meant to be an archetypal personification of elemental man; and, as such, he is more than adequate. Perhaps he is not intellectual enough to be fairly representative of Italian culture and to be an archetypal figure in this sense. His depths are emotional, not intellectual. If he symbolizes Italy, there are dimensions to the country, we feel, which he does not adequately mirror.

Where Angels Fear to Tread is a subtle, complex, and refreshing novel; and, in its total impact, it justifies the opinion that Forster was from the first an artist of maturity and power. The same judgment is true of *A Room with a View*, which also analyzes the influence of Italy on the staid British character.

II "*A Sense of Deities Reconciled*": A Room with a View

Forster began *A Room with a View* (1908) before *Where Angels Fear to Tread* (1905) and finished it after *The Longest Journey* (1907). In *Where Angels Fear to Tread*, Italy had been the sole source of vitality. Italy acts similarly in *A Room with a View*, but so does rural England. Italy retreats to the background, but still acts as a formative influence after the characters return to England in Part II. It is the main force which in Part I contributes to Lucy Honeychurch's liberation. The conventional Reverend Beebe reluctantly acknowledges the intuitive wisdom of Italians: "They pry everywhere, they see everything, and they know what we want before we know it ourselves" (39). So "Phaethon," the driver of the carriage taking the English to the hills above Florence, reads Lucy's heart and directs her to George Emerson rather than to the clergyman when she asks in faltering Italian "where the good man is." Both Italy and the English countryside encourage a free and open existence as compared to cramped, stereotyped, middle-class social life. The primary impression produced by the novel, the prevalence of wind and air and sunlight, at once recalls the fiction of Meredith and establishes the primary role of nature as a redemptive power.

The English and Italian settings, rendered with complete immediacy, reveal Forster's sensitivity to place. Houses and buildings take on life in his fiction: the church of Santa Croce and the Pension Bertolini in Florence, for example, and Windy Corner, a Sussex country house. The Florentine pension and the Sussex house focus the action in the two sections of the novel. Chapter 1 presents at the Pension Bertolini almost all the actors who figure in Part I: Lucy; Charlotte Bartlett, her "proper" chaperone; George Emerson, a sad but vital young man; his father, the prophetic advocate of the free and natural life; Mr. Beebe, the ascetically inclined but agreeable clergyman who presides at Windy Corner; and Eleanor Lavish, an "emancipated" novelist whose unconventionality is superficial. Only the Misses Alan and the malicious chaplain to the English colony, the Reverend Cuthbert Eager, remain for Chapters 2 and 3. The opening chapter of Part II introduces at Windy Corner all the other principals: Mrs. Honeychurch, Lucy's impulsive but shrewd mother; Freddy, Lucy's playful but instinctively sound brother; and Cecil Vyse, a "medieval" young man to whom Lucy has become engaged after his third proposal to her. Lucy and George return for their honeymoon to the Pension Bertolini in the concluding chapter which provides a frame for the novel and a reminder of Italy's pervasive power.

Structure depends upon a number of encounters between Lucy and George which revise her staid outlook. In Chapter 1, the Emersons offer the ladies their room with a view; and before retiring the now restless Lucy gazes beyond the Arno at the hills which betoken a freedom that she has not yet achieved. In Chapter 2, George appears in the church of Santa Croce at his most lugubrious; and Lucy disdainfully pities him; in Chapter 4, George supports her in his arms when she faints from witnessing a quarrel between two Italians over money, a quarrel that results in murder. After Lucy's "rescue," she and George gaze at the Arno flowing beneath them and respond to its mystery and promise; and they do so again when they go back to Florence for their honeymoon.

Violence enlarges Lucy's horizons, and she now feels that something has indeed "happened to the living." Chapter 4 also suggests the effete quality of the ordinary tourists' culture when Lucy buys photographs of the great masters. Reality impinges upon the pictures when the dying man's blood spatters them and when George throws them into the Arno to have them washed pure in its waters. The principal picture, Botticelli's "The Birth of Venus," has symbolic meaning that is at once lucid and profound. The picture connects with the Italian springtime, the pagan atmosphere of the novel, and the birth of love in Lucy's soul. Just as the blood of the murdered man defiles the pictures, so Lucy would, through her own blindness and obstinacy, do violence to her instincts. Just as the soiled photographs return to the water that has given birth in legend to the goddess of love, so Lucy must immerse herself in the most elemental of passions in order to cleanse her soul and to attain a new life. The birth of the goddess and the death of the Italian man also suggest the nearness of love and death as the most significant and mysterious of experiences.

Another encounter with George occurs when the Bertolini guests go for a drive above Fiesole in Chapter 6. Lucy now discovers that her standards have altered and that she does not know how to account for the change. She doubts that Miss Lavish is an

artist and that Mr. Beebe is spiritual, but previously she would
have been less critical. She judges them by a new criterion; vital
energy should animate them, she thinks. But she finds them lacking in warmth and spontaneity, qualities that she has begun un-
consciously to associate with George. Lucy is a woman who
registers the effects of an emotional awakening before she can acknowledge its existence and cause. The Arno Valley is once more
present in the distance from above Fiesole when George kisses
Lucy after she surprises him on the violet-covered bank during
this excursion.

Encounters with George also organize the narrative in Part II,
although in the first chapters it is Cecil Vyse, Lucy's fiancé (or
"fiasco" as Freddy calls him) who dominates. Another kiss, Cecil's
self-conscious embrace in Chapter 9, contrasts with George's
spontaneous caresses. Cecil not only takes temporarily the place
of George as his temperamental opposite, but assumes in Part II
the role of Charlotte Bartlett as an exemplar of the proprieties. In
Chapter 12 Lucy regains contact with George as he emerges from
"The Sacred Lake," a charming woodland pool in Sussex, and
emanates all of nature's freshness.

Part II is a contest between George and Cecil for the control of
Lucy's inner being. In Chapter 15, a kiss again enlivens the novel.
George has just beaten Lucy at tennis; and, while the contestants
rest, Cecil reads from Miss Lavish's novel. The book, which has
Italy for setting, features an incident similar to George's first kiss
on the heights over Florence. The memory of this scene arouses
George's passion, and he kisses the woman he loves in a copse
close to Windy Corner. Lucy, who is outraged, again does violence to her true self; she retreats from the light of truth and passion and prepares to enter "the vast armies of the benighted"
(204). After this second kiss and the lies she tells about herself to
George, Cecil, Mr. Beebe, her mother, and Mr. Emerson, pretense
conquers her. In Florence after George's kiss she had realized how
difficult it was to be truthful, but by this point she has become less
conscientious.

The overall movement of the novel results in enlightenment for
Lucy, after several divagations into falsehood. With one side of
her nature, she responds to passion as it concenters in George;
with another, she aligns herself with upholders of Victorian social
standards, Charlotte Bartlett and Cecil Vyse. With unremitting

force, Lucy's instincts carry her toward a larger life than these others will allow her before she breaks free of their influence. Finally, Mr. Emerson sweeps away her accumulated falsities when he divines her love for George, lectures her on the sanctity of passion, and gives her the courage to claim the man she loves.

In Italy, Lucy's well-known world breaks up; and in its place there is the "magic city" of Florence where people think and do the unusual and the unpredictable. Passionate, vibrant, violent Italy all but overwhelms her. She is startled, for one thing, by her sympathies with "Phaethon" when he embraces his "Persephone" on the drive to Fiesole. If she had seen more clearly, she would have recognized a god in George Emerson, who would, for his part, have seen in a liberated Lucy his counterpart. Before he kissed her in the hills, she had seemed indeed "as one who had fallen out of heaven" (80); and, before her inhibitions asserted themselves, Lucy identified George with "heroes—gods—the nonsense of schoolgirls" (85). Later, when she greets him near the Sacred Lake, she thinks of herself as bowing "to gods, to heroes, to the nonsense of school girls! She had bowed across the rubbish that cumbers the world" (155). And George was here a "Michelangelesque" figure, the essence of heroic vitality; earlier he had appeared to Lucy as a figure appropriate to "the ceiling of the Sistine Chapel, carrying a burden of acorns" (29). But, in repudiating George a second time, she turns from a god incarnate to the academic study of Greek mythology as she prepares for her journey to Greece with the Misses Alan. She fails to perceive that she is rejecting in the actuality a god, knowledge of whose counterparts she is pursuing in the abstract.

In order to intensify Lucy's conflict with authority and to convey the force of her buried passion, Forster uses imagery based on music.[4] Music lifts her out of herself and permits her to see truly the irrelevance of her prescriptive standards: "She was then no longer either deferential or patronizing; no longer either a rebel or a slave" (34). By force of will, she transforms Beethoven's tragic sonatas, for example, into expressions of triumph. But Lucy instinctively suits her music to her mood or situation. In Italy where primitive passion survives, she leans toward Beethoven. When she plays for Cecil and his guests in London, she performs Schumann, who suggests to her "the sadness of the incomplete." It is as if she half realizes, in some recess of her being, that she is denying the demands of life, and so cannot play her beloved Beethoven in these artificial surroundings. When she plans to renounce the call of passion, she indulges in the artifice (for her) of Mozart.

Forster suggests Lucy's progress toward enlightenment in terms of light and shadow images, images so numerous that I cannot discuss them in detail. Light and darkness suffuse natural phenomena, as these may signify freedom and spiritual fulfillment or bondage and human perversity. Forster also associates light with the Emersons to the extent that father and son represent spiritual truth. In Italy, Mr. Emerson instructs Lucy to bring up her thoughts to the sunlight from the depths of her nature. She resists full illumination, however, because she denies the sacred promptings of instinct. George is, like Lucy, in danger of the abyss. He will enter obscurity if Lucy does not return his love, his father asserts; and Lucy will condemn herself by her evasions to "marching in the armies of darkness" (212).

Though the clouds of pessimism often surround George, he becomes a source of light to Lucy. Both darkness and bright light characterize her encounter with him in the Piazza Signoria. To correspond with the crime that takes place there, the Piazza is in shadow and the tower of the palace arises out of sinister gloom. Yet the tower is emblematic of the sexuality which Lucy experiences there and represses, rising as it does "out of the lower darkness like a pillar of roughened gold. It seemed no longer a tower, no longer supported by earth, but some unattainable treasure throbbing in the tranquil sky" (48).

In Sussex, George's kindness to his father strikes Lucy as "sunlight touching a vast landscape—a touch of the morning sun" (177). He has just said that "there is a certain amount of kindness, just as there is a certain amount of light," and that one "should stand in it for all you are worth, facing the sunshine." When he wins at tennis from Lucy, he is brilliant against the sunlight, godlike in appearance. In defending himself in Sussex after he kisses her, he emphasizes how his love had been kindled when he saw her the day he bathed in the Sacred Lake; the life-giving water combined with the glorious sunlight to make her beauty overwhelming. It is with this sunlight, too, that Forster identifies George and suggests that he is a Phaethon figure.

After she breaks the engagement with Cecil, Lucy realizes that George has gone into darkness; but she does not yet perceive that by her denial of sex she is fashioning an "armor of falsehood" (186) and is about to go into darkness herself. She now becomes as one who sins "against passion and truth" (204), or against Eros and Pallas Athena. She also resists taking others into confidence lest inner exploration result in self-knowledge and "that king of terrors—Light" (225). But for the intervention of Mr. Emerson, Lucy would remain in darkness. He gives her "a sense of deities reconciled" (240); he enables her, in short, to balance the claims of Eros and Pallas Athena, of sense and soul.

George, who is in part a nature god, is seen at his most vital against the expanse of Florentine and Sussex hills. Appropriately enough, his earliest memory is the inspiriting landscape seen from Hindhead in company with his mother and father, a prospect which seemed to unify the family in the deepest understanding. In symbolic terms, both the Emersons now have, and have always had, "the view" which Lucy must acquire. External nature is always seen in motion as if it also is in protest against Cecil's static existence and in sympathy with George's dynamic energies. Kinetic and auditory images dominate so that nature seems always an active rather than a passive force. The Arno River after a storm bounds on like a lion, and at several points it murmurs a promise of a free and open existence for the lovers. In Sussex, the atmosphere, comprising "the intolerable tides of heaven" (94), is always in motion. Glorious lateral views dominate the country; but this landscape becomes ominous as Lucy represses her natural passions. The sounds and movements of nature intensify to register their protest as Lucy denies life and love. Now the sky goes wild; the winds roar through the groaning pine trees; and gray clouds, charging across the heavens, obscure the white ones and the blue sky, "as the roaring tides of darkness" set in. The novel closes on a halcyon note, however, with nature's forces finding fruition in human beings, as Lucy on her honeymoon surrenders to the Florentine Spring and to the Arno's whispers.

When Mr. Emerson counsels Lucy toward the novel's end, he emphasizes the difficulties of life, the continual presence of muddles, and the consequent need for us to clear them away; he quotes a friend of his to the effect that, "Life is a public performance on the violin, in which you must learn the instrument as you go along" (236). Like Caroline Abbott and Philip Herriton, Lucy acquires a sense of the complexities of life; and she finds that she

cannot plan for it and know its contingencies in advance. This
lesson she learns from her first meeting with George in Sussex, for
she had not thought of meeting him in a happy mood, as a godlike
creature against the background of verdant nature.

In spite of the artistry with which Forster analyzes her development, Lucy is not very impressive; and her conflicts and perceptions are somewhat meager. Perhaps her stature is diminished by
Forster's failure to establish the Emersons, her mentors, as fully
differentiated creations. Virtually all of Forster's critics have had
some reservations about these two men.

George is even less complex than Lucy and much less fully analyzed. He has heroic vitality and youthful energy, and he loves
sincerely and passionately. But he lacks Lucy's intelligence and
her capacity to develop. He functions inadequately in this novel,
therefore, especially since some kind of transcendent significance
supposedly inheres in his marriage to Lucy. To this meaning,
George contributes little. Although George gives Lucy "the feeling of greyness, of tragedy that might only find solution in the
night" (29), Forster never establishes the intellectual grounds for
George's pessimism. His fatalism is too conscious a *weltschmerz* to
be interesting and has no inevitable basis in his experience. As an
archetypal presence, he is too slight a figure to register forcibly.

Even more disastrous to positive effect is Mr. Emerson, a disciple of Samuel Butler. Forster conceives him with less decisive-
ness and complexity than the novel demands, his valetudinarian-
ism is too far removed from the vitality attributed to him, and his
message is too direct for it to be esthetically compelling. But what
damages Mr. Emerson chiefly is the dated quality of his ideas,
ideas which reveal how shallow he is when he assumes that he is
being profound. In his scathing remarks about the Reverend Eager's Giotto lecture in the Church of Santa Croce, Mr. Emerson
exhibits a literalness of mind not far different from the fundamen-
talism he criticizes. Thus he asserts that an edifice built by faith
means that the workmen were underpaid and that Giotto's "As-
cension of Saint John" is ridiculous because a "fat man in blue"
could not be "shooting into the sky like an air-balloon" (27). It is
therefore difficult to agree with Forster that Mr. Emerson is "pro-
foundly religious," for he seems to operate on the surface, rather
than at the depths, of spiritual issues.

Forster's great success in the novel is with his rendition of the humorous and satirically envisioned persons. Some of them—the Reverend Eager, Mrs. Honeychurch, and Eleanor Lavish—Forster presents in brief, through epigrammatic summary or through their spoken words. Forster tells us, for instance, all we have to know of Reverend Eager, by describing briefly his unctuous ministrations for transient visitors: ". . . it was his avowed custom to select those of his migratory sheep who seemed worthy, and give them a few hours in the pastures of the permanent" (59). The portrait is made complete when Eager discourses patronizingly upon the way in which the "lower class" Emersons have risen: "Generally, one has only sympathy for their success. The desire for education and for social advance—in these things there is something not wholly vile. There are some working men whom one would be very willing to see out here in Florence—little as they would make of it" (62). Reverend Eager's remarks reveal a generosity more apparent than real; actually, they mask feelings of snobbishness, contempt, and exclusiveness.

But it is with Lucy's antagonists that Forster does best: Charlotte Bartlett and Cecil Vyse. Although he presents them satirically, he also sees them sympathetically; as a result, his humor at their expense is genial as well as satiric. Charlotte and Cecil are misguided, they are hypocrites, and they extinguish the generous instincts; they cause unhappiness and they propagate darkness. But, since they are not conscious of wrongdoing, Forster not only tolerates them but feels affection for them. As a consequence, he fully delineates them; and they become large-scale figures even if they are not complex individuals who develop dynamically.

Charlotte is given to excessive propriety and is deficient, therefore, in graciousness, kindness, and consideration. Her hypocrisies are, of course, the source of much fine comedy, as is her penchant for the irrelevant. Specious and superficial incidents and ideas gain ascendancy in her mind and allow her thereby to evade uncomfortable realities which a conscientious individual would feel obliged to face. She is able to rationalize any occurrence in her own favor. Thus she stresses Miss Lavish's perfidy in using for her novel Lucy's encounter with George. As a result, Charlotte diverts attention from her own perfidy in telling Miss Lavish in the first place: "Never again shall Eleanor Lavish be a friend of mine" (191). Her incompetence as a person who is "practical without ability" is the source of much humor. Her packing in Florence is protracted further than it ought to be; she is unable to pay the driver at Windy Corner because she arrives without change and then becomes confused in her monetary calculations; and she "impedes Mrs. Honeychurch with her assistance" when she ties up dahlias after a night of storm.

The portrait of Cecil is equally authoritative. He is the diffident man who finds it difficult to become emotionally involved even with an attractive woman. Forster describes him as resembling a "fastidious saint" in the façade of a French cathedral and as being by temperament self-conscious and ascetic. His courtship follows the arc from "patronizing civility" to a "profound uneasiness." The uneasiness arises when Lucy threatens to become vital and dynamic, to be more than a Leonardesque work of art.

George Emerson appraises well his adversary. He perceives that Cecil "kills," when it comes to people, by misjudging or undervaluing them, by playing tricks on them instead of cherishing "the most sacred form of life that he can find" (194). For this reason Cecil patronizes Lucy when she confuses two Italian painters; winces when Mr. Emerson mispronounces the names of painters; seems to sneer as the Honeychurches go to church; is bored and disdainful of the Honeychurches for whom "eggs, boilers, hydrangeas, maids" form part of reality; and cannot see that it is sometimes an act of kindness for a bad player to make a fourth at tennis. In short, as with Meredith's Sir Willoughby Patterne, Cecil is an egoist, with the egoist's inability to see himself as he is, with the egoist's tendency to assume that other people exist to minister to his well-being. Something of the large dimensions of Sir Willoughby inhere in Cecil's portrait, but Lucy Honeychurch seems small beside Clara Middleton, her prototype in Meredith.

III Forster's "Natural Supernaturalism": The Tales

While Forster was composing his first four novels, he also wrote short stories. They are almost all delicate, sometimes self-conscious ventures into fantasy, a mode which Forster used intermittently in his novels. In discussing the short stories we should ascertain, therefore, the point where realism and fantasy merge most authoritatively, the point where the "something extra" which fantasy exacts is most willingly conceded (*Aspects of the Novel*, 109). Such a fusion of the here and now with the intimations of the imagination Forster found in Lewis Carroll: " . . . fantasy slides into daily life, everyday life into fantasy, without a jerk, without the waving of a wand." [5] The finest tales illustrate this skilled fusion of realism and fantasy, but the weaker ones do not always attain it.

In "Mr. Andrews," "Co-ordination," and "The Machine Stops," Forster fails to dramatize conclusively his complex and original concepts.[6] These tales tend to be patent allegories and to lack substance and weight as a result. His tendency in them—to rely almost totally upon fantasy—provides only tentative support for the values which he explores through personality and incident. Actual substance in "The Other Side of the Hedge" is also slighter than animating idea. The theme—that few men are willing to embrace a spirited self-sufficiency—is much more challenging in the abstract than it is memorably embodied in Forster's parable.

"Other Kingdom" and "The Story of a Panic" are more authentic weldings of the realistic and the supernatural. Realistic detail secures credence for Forster's departures from the empirically verifiable—that is, for his resort to fantasy. A narrator whose simplicity or imperceptiveness prevents a sure assessment of his experience is an interesting, if not altogether successful, technical innovation in these stories. Such a narrator is usually unable to distinguish between his illusions and the reality; and this disparity often enables Forster to present his own values by implication or by ironic contrasts. Since these intelligences are inadequate for judging the truth, the reader must make his own discriminations, using ideas expressed elsewhere by Forster or conveyed tangentially within the stories.

"Other Kingdom" obliquely analyzes the effects produced by a conventional, ruthless man, Harcourt Worters, upon his sensitive, elfin fiancée Evelyn Beaumont. The painfulness of her suffering after marriage implies that she acquiesces only partly in his views. Her escape from him, then, is foreordained; and the extremity of her metamorphosis into a dryad, inhabiting one of her beloved trees, is related necessarily to her total aversion to him. By this transformation Forster gains peace for Evelyn and suitable justice for a relentless husband—the loss of one whom he appreciates as an object rather than as a spirit. There follows the ironic spectacle of a forceful man bent upon revenge whose plans come to nothing because he is set against forces too powerful and subtle for him to understand, much less control to his advantage. He is the antithe-

sis of the self-sufficient Ford (Evelyn's friend), whose insight is as
unerring as his human sympathy is complete.

"The Story of a Panic" develops a similar contrast between the
conventional and the spontaneous, but this time one individual
confronts a group of imperceptive people. One of these, the narrator, is aggravated by the unusual events which he must recount
but cannot comprehend. The superiority of Eustace to the other
English with him at Ravello is implied when he alone does not
panic as a "catspaw" of wind, betokening the arrival of Pan, blows
upon them at an upland picnic. He acknowledges in a flash of
vision the god who stirs the deepest currents of his nature. Gen-
naro, who, Judas-like, betrays Eustace to his English guardians
for silver, later dies like Christ for his friend when the English try
to prevent Eustace's escape from confinement in the hotel—escape from constricted modern life to a free existence with the
great god Pan. Mythological and Christian allusions, poetry of setting, and an ironic removal of Eustace's tragedy from the narrator's sympathy engender dimensions of meaning deeper than
those in the stories I have already discussed.

In "The Road from Colonus," "The Eternal Moment," "The
Story of the Siren," and "The Point of It," Forster combined, more
successfully still, the actual with the purely imaginative; and he
achieved an increased degree of credence for these works. In evocation of atmosphere, in subtle analysis of the conflicts within personality, in penetration to the depths of consciousness, and in fusion of character with situation, they represent his most notable
successes as a story writer. Fantasy is all the stronger for being
indirectly evoked, and it helps bring into being the dreamlike atmosphere suffusing these tales and the authentic revelation in
them of "Truths that wake/To perish never."

In "The Road from Colonus," the most haunting and powerful
of all the tales, Forster uses myth ironically and satirically to give
his story amplitude. Mr. Lucas just misses the tragic stature of a
dying Oedipus through the officiousness of his daughter and survives to a querulous, instead of a dignified, old age. Ethel Lucas is
an Antigone-like guardian of her father but is concerned only for
his physical well-being, not for his soul. Toward the end of a dis-
couraging expedition in Greece, Mr. Lucas visits a huge votive
tree, inside whose hollow trunk he feels his soul expand, as he
gazes upon the redemptive stream flowing through it. He experi-

ences a kinship with the timeless energies of nature; and, in his moment of vision, he discovers the truth not only about Greece but about England and the whole of life.

From this supreme moment of transfiguration, his daughter drags him away. As it turns out, that same night during a storm the votive tree fell upon the inn in which he had wished to stay, killing all the people in it. Mr. Lucas's later desiccation in London, the result of his apathetic existence, is more terrible by far than certain death would have been had he been able to stay in rural Greece as he had wished. The inner life, Forster implies, reaches a maximum fullness, as it did for Mr. Lucas at Colonus; and it disintegrates thereafter if sustenance is denied it. Unless we are free to revive the precious visionary moment, or strong enough to remember it, it will perish as if it had never been.

Forster enlarges in "The Eternal Moment" upon the moral power exerted by the "symbolic moment" and the momentous effects which may follow its denial. Miss Raby finally faces the truth about herself even when this act disrupts the security she might have enjoyed in her last years. She perceives that her rejection of sex meant deterioration for a man who then dedicated himself to money instead of love. Her courage is more admirable than her insight into social realities; her honesty is disruptive even if it allows her to achieve a self-catharsis.

Miss Raby's celebration of Vorta in her first novel brought a rush of tourists to devastate the town's beauty. Thus she discovers two truths: our actions have infinite consequences; and the moment is eternal only for those with courage, foresight, and force enough to grasp it. She has had the strength to cherish the moment in memory; and from its transfiguring influence all that is worthwhile for her derived, at the same time that she may have missed the best in life by playing the shocked lady when a boy had been on fire with love for her. She feels, however, that she has lived consistently and "worthily," even if she has never known completeness of being. But we as readers know, as she does also, that her moment has by now become a faded memory and has ceased to be much of a vital impulse for her present existence.[7] The mythological and fantastic are in abeyance in this tale except as Forster's imagination raises to its true—and greater than normal—proportions a significant incident from Miss Raby's past.

Myth and fantasy arc primary elements in "The Story of the

Siren." The Sicilian boy who tells about the siren has a scapegrace brother, a kind of devil's disciple who alone in the village sees the siren and becomes unsettled as a result of this confrontation with naked reality. His wife goes mad after her encounter with the siren. The child to be born to them, it is rumored, will be Antichrist; and will raise up the siren and restore the world. Accordingly, a Christian priest, acting from a fear that is not Christian, pushes the woman from a cliff before her son can be born. The Christian community that concurs in the priest's deed fails to see that the greatest sin perhaps is to do evil that good may supposedly result. By her equanimity the siren implicitly condemns human fears and hatreds and the village's lack of Christian charity. When the siren will rise, the baleful power of institutional Christianity will end; and she will "sing, destroy silence, primness, and cruelty, and save the world." [8]

The story assimilates its unusual incidents in a number of ways. First, there is the contrast between the conventional, academic first-person narrator and the Sicilian boy. By this means, Forster dramatizes the impingement of a primitive, still fitfully surviving pagan world upon a "normal" individual who is deficient in imagination. The boy also fears the siren as much as he believes in her, and thereby he makes of her a tangible influence in his own life. He attains only momentary peace of mind since she is a sinister as well as a reassuring reality to him. The source of much of the story's strength is the implication that the siren is to be equated with a moral reality which transcends good and evil. She symbolizes, therefore, the difficult truth that men must face if they are to be wholly free. Thus mythology in the story serves metaphysical as well as purely esthetic ends.

"The Point of It" is as noteworthy for the rendition of ideas central in Forster as it is for establishing a credible supernatural atmosphere. The central character, Micky, is a "cultured" man whose inner life is meaningless because it has been so precisely settled at its outset. Theme and meaning in "The Point of It" are best defined through structure, which evinces both a progression as Micky is enlightened and a return to the circumstances of youth when he has acquired wisdom. Micky, however, does not attain awareness until after his death.

In the first scene, Micky is guarding his friend Harold, who has been sent to the seaside to recuperate from overexertion. Alarmed at Harold's frenzied rowing, Micky confesses that he does not quite see the point of such effort. Harold replies that Micky some day will see "the point of it" and forthwith dies from an over-strained heart. The twofold point eludes Micky for some fifty years: his own life never reached a higher intensity than in Harold's company, and Harold—in precipitate yielding to instinct—had achieved an even more exalted ecstasy, which opened out for him the utmost possibilities to be reached by the self. Until the final movement of the tale, Micky fails to attain the truths which he had once almost grasped, that intuition is superior to the unaided intellect and that one must be pure in heart to grasp the beatific vision. The only person who remotely approaches Harold in vitality is Micky's son, Adam, for whom Micky, in complacent mid-career, develops an unconquerable aversion.

This short "life-in-life" sequence at the seacoast is succeeded by a longer sequence recounting Micky's death-in-life as a prosperous, smug civil servant. His pale humanism cannot withstand the genuineness of violence: he has no reserves to fall back upon, for example, after he encounters the two slum women who quarrel over a large fish and hit him a great blow with it when he intervenes, violence that causes his death.

The third movement is a death-in-death sequence in hell, although Micky now becomes aware of his faults and is thereby prepared for redemption. Death-in-death continues for some time because at first Micky reacts to hell with apathy rather than with an active desire to change his situation. A spirit—no doubt Harold or his ghost—now comes to disturb the apathetic dwellers beyond the river Acheron by its singing. Of the shades on the plain, Micky is the only one to be converted by this Unseen presence because he alone wishes to remember his ignoble past with a view to reordering it.

Micky now comes to a phase of life-in-death in which he learns that ultimate reality resides in the sheer desire for strength and beauty. Micky's second "death" takes place—his being born into Eternity—and it is accompanied by terrible pain as he faces the reality which he had previously disregarded. Once Micky says that he desires light, the counseling Spirit vanishes; and he finds himself back in the boat where he had been years ago with Harold. Micky has at last found "the point of it"—as Harold had promised he would,—that a man can save himself only by a desire

to retain, or to reach, spiritual purity and ecstasy. The reverbera-
tions of significance in the story demonstrate Forster's intrepid
fusion of social commentary and esthetic inventiveness. This
union of the critically acute and the imaginatively ingenious is, in
fact, the chief excellence of his short stories, as it also tends to be
of his novels.

CHAPTER 3

"The Union of Shadow and Adamant":
The Longest Journey

I Rickie Elliot and the Life of the Imagination

*T*HE *Longest Journey* (1907) is the most tantalizing and elusive of Forster's narratives. Most Forsterians would modify John Harvey's unfavorable estimate in his 1956 article, but they would be unable to deny the flaws which he documents: the unmotivated deaths; the arbitrary nature of some of the symbolism; the high-pitched emotionalism in some scenes; and the uncertainty which sometimes obtrudes in the characters because they must at once illustrate, positively or negatively, Forster's own values and be embodiments of the complexities of actual human nature. On the credit side are merits which distinguish the fiction as a whole: a brisk narrative pace, a poetic yet precise style, a piquant humor, an unusual angle of vision, an eloquent descriptive power, an evocative symbolism, an elemental quality in the people and the action, and a sure sense, frequently, of psychological motivation.

Forster further accounts for the imaginative power exerted in the book when he confesses that the protagonist, Rickie Elliot, is his most autobiographical character. The solicitude with which he analyzes Rickie and his retreat from the light reveals Forster's own identification with him. When, on the ride over the downs to Salisbury, Rickie realizes the ephemeral and perhaps fruitless lives of those myriads who have lived and died in this region, Forster implies that Rickie's reactions have their universal implications. Some of us, he asserts, have Rickie's qualities of temperament, repeat his experiences, and acknowledge their truth. Rickie may see certain aspects of reality with less clarity than do some other characters; still, he arouses our interest more consistently, since as McConkey explains (37), he tries to do more by assimilating the best features of several approaches to life. He is, besides, fallibly human; and his mistakes derive from frailty, not viciousness of nature. The equanimity and justice of his standards compel even his hostile aunt, Emily Failing, to admit that he is the true heir of her deceased husband, Tony, the wisest character in the novel, even though he figures in it only as a voice from the dead and was sometimes ineffectual when he was alive.

Like the other humanists in the novel (his friend Stewart Ansell and his dead uncle Tony Failing), Rickie continually tries to define for himself the nature of ultimate reality, although this quest may never be completed. To his detriment, Rickie tends to distrust the concrete as opposed to the idealizing of it. Rickie's romantic imagination, however, provides his greatest strength and weakness; his initial values are not so much mistaken as seen too often in an uncritical perspective. He is, furthermore, subject to attack by people more masterful than he; and he does not always know how, therefore, to hold fast to the best of his perceptions. Through Rickie, Forster projects the beauties and potential rewards of the imaginative life, as well as its potential dangers.

Because Rickie would rather examine his own mind than argue in support of his own ideas, he does not participate actively in the opening discussion. He is too diffident, possibly too skeptical, to have formed definite views about the "reality" of the cow; at the same time, he is too poetical by instinct to do much with pure logic. He senses that reality is neither so "ideal" as Stewart Ansell insists nor so empiric as Tilliard maintains. Rather, Rickie feels that elms are neither solid objects, independent of the individual's sensibility, nor insubstantial phenomena, lurking only at the borders of our minds. He believes that elms may be dryads, and he develops for himself a reality at once concrete and ideal. Forster, in fact, suggests that "the line between the two is subtler than we admit" (12). But judging by the ultimate success of his stories, we perceive that his poetic insight is sharper than Ansell's and subtler than Stephen's, even if some of his intellectual formulations are suspect.

Despite the claims of Ansell's ideal world, one would do well not to stray too far from the concrete. If the objects in our world have a spiritual as well as a substantial basis, we should nevertheless regard critically any abstractions built upon them. This is the gist of the famous discussion in Chapter 28, which comes at the end of the second movement ("Sawston") and balances the opening chapters of the first movement ("Cambridge") about the nature of the cow's reality. In this chapter Forster emphasizes in direct commentary the pernicious aspects of an imagination which departs too radically and inflexibly from the truth inherent in our empirical perceptions. The opening discussion and Forster's delayed commentary thus reinforce each other: one cannot truthfully know his own soul until he has gained some knowledge of the world. The only sane program, as Forster said elsewhere, is for us to "hate worldliness, but love the world." [1]

Visitors for Rickie interrupt this discussion, Agnes Pembroke and her brother Herbert. Ansell, for whom reality is mental, rudely disregards Agnes since for him she does not exist as a real person. Shortly after the visit, Agnes' lover, Gerald Dawes, dies in a football match; and she turns for comfort to Rickie. Love develops, and over Ansell's protest Rickie marries. He undertakes "the longest journey" with an uncongenial mate for whom he must give up his friends and genuine interests. Physically, Rickie is no match for the overbearing Gerald, and he fails to dominate his wife. In turn, Agnes is selfish, unimaginative, and materialistic.

Rickie is also false to his deepest self when as teacher he adopts Herbert's standards at Sawston School and when he is led, at Agnes' behest, to deny the claims upon him of his half-brother, Stephen Wonham. Mrs. Failing had revealed to Rickie, in a moment of pique, Stephen's identity when the engaged couple visited her at Cadover house in Wiltshire. Rickie then assumed that Stephen is the bastard child of his hated father. Not until after his marriage to Agnes and Mrs. Failing expels Stephen from Cadover, does Rickie learn, through Ansell, that Stephen is the illegitimate son of his mother. Mrs. Elliot had been the victim of her husband's cruelty and had turned to Robert, a Wiltshire farmer and man of the soil, for release. The lovers eloped to Sweden where Stephen was conceived and Robert drowned. When Mrs. Elliot was forced to return to her hated husband, Stephen became the adopted child of the Failings.

Once Rickie learns the total truth about Stephen, he has the courage to repudiate Agnes and join his brother. On a journey back to Wiltshire, the two reach a deep accord when they sail flame boats down a stream near Cadover. This harmony is shattered, however, after Stephen breaks his promise to Rickie not to drink. Rickie comes upon his drunken brother just in time to rescue him at the local crossing but is himself run over by the oncoming train. After Rickie's death, Stephen marries and cherishes his brother's memory by naming his child after their mother; and he also acknowledges that Rickie's money has made possible his own free life upon the beloved Wiltshire acres.

Rickie starts with a truth which he later denies and to which he still later returns. Metaphysical finality derives from the coloring given to our perceptions by the modulating reason—or the disciplined imagination—not from the exclusive exercise of either senses or intellect. The most illuminating glimpses of the truth, then, must depart from a strict empiricism, though one must never depart completely from it; or, as Forster himself says in his analysis of him, Rickie "came to his worthier results rather by imagination and instinct than by logic" (191). I therefore agree with J. B. Beer who—in *The Achievement of E. M. Forster* (1962)—regards Rickie as a positive as well as a passive individual (78, 90). Rickie has thus his moment of truth in his inability to side with either the empiricists like Tilliard or the Berkeleyans like Ansell. Rather, Rickie sees that imagination must transform the world of sensation for that world to achieve fullness of meaning. The disciplined imagination, in short, elicits, or reinforces, the ideal properties latent in the objects we perceive.

In light of this principle, Rickie composes his stories by subjecting his sense impressions to the impress of fantasy. Late in his Cambridge career, after he falls in love with Agnes, he tends, however, to discount imagination; and he values too highly his disparate, specific experiences. At this point he asks himself this question: "When real things are so wonderful, what is the point of pretending?" (74). At times, Rickie lets his own imagination riot; for the moment, he is guilty of the opposite error of distrusting it too completely. If, at its best, his imagination transfigures the mundane, making something new and arresting from it, at this time Rickie ceases to linger "on gods and heroes, on the infinite and the impossible, on virtue and beauty and strength" (74). He rejects the ideas and aspirations which give strength to his mind, and he focuses instead upon the actual individual who is Agnes.

The reality inheres in concretions, but its furthest ramifications are visionary and only intermittently to be apprehended. Furthermore, it can never be fully defined or exhausted. Ansell's quaint exercise in the concentric patterning of squares and circles—of fashioning each time "a new symbol for the universe, a fresh circle within the square" (211)—now gathers new meaning. If, as he maintains, the figure farthest inside is the real one, its outlines lose identity as its significance intensifies. Accordingly, final reality is as difficult to perceive as it is to pinpoint. As George H. Thomson asserts in *The Fiction of E. M. Forster* (1967), the inmost figure is the circle and it links with the other circle images such as the Cadbury Rings in Wiltshire and the British Museum dome (141ff.), which act as expansive symbols in the novel.

At the same time, the most commonplace object may open out to proclaim that the infinite lies within it. This is partly the significance of Ansell's striking matches when the cow's substantial or ideal nature is debated. The brands of wood, lit by flame, are symbols of a circumambient infinity present, here and now, in the solid objects which we perceive. Near the novel's end, the paper balls, lit by Stephen into mystic roses of flame and sent through the bridge arches, are also symbols of the supernatural emanating from, and controlled within, the natural. Rickie loses sight of his flaming rose before Stephen does; the over-spreading life-force will die out from him but be preserved through Stephen's children.

In the end, the imagination which allows Rickie to achieve much misleads him. An excess of enthusiasm causes him to misinterpret the embrace of Gerald and Agnes as a paradisiacal attachment and to see in Agnes a spiritual dimension which she does not possess. He is thereby false to the genuine imagination which at times gives him his extraordinary perceptions. One bitter irony which Beer (88) singles out is that Rickie's imagination is stimulated by a girl who herself has none. His romanticizing of Gerald as a Greek out of Aristophanes reveals critical powers in abeyance; he forgets what he had only just been reminded of, Gerald's brutality when they were both at school.

After Gerald's death, Agnes becomes for Rickie, in Ansell's view, "a single peg" upon which to hang "all the world's beauty" (96). He sees her, as if with the vision of Blake, "a virgin widow, tall, veiled, consecrated" (72). For him, she becomes a transcendent being, a Beatrice, a Clara Middleton, a Brunhilde, "a light . . . suddenly held behind the world" (99) to enlighten his existence. The light she effuses, however, is not really warm and life-infusing; it is, as Widdrington explains, the brisk glare induced when an electric light clicks on. In practice Rickie's idealism flour-

ishes at the expense of his sense of fact; tragically for him, he falls
in love "through the imagination" rather than "through the desires." A vision, we infer, can mislead as well as illuminate. For,
despite Agnes' imposing beauty and brusque good nature, she is
superficial, devious, sadistic, and sometimes barbaric in aspect
and action. Only gradually do her Philistinism and vindictiveness
become apparent to Rickie: when he sees her for what she is, his
life with her seems as unreal as the grotesque sheep engraved
upon their domestic accounts book. She leads him away from his
true moral bent, especially after Mrs. Failing's revelation that Stephen is his half-brother. Because she prevents him from acknowledging Stephen, she is the Eve to Rickie's Adam, as McConkey
points out (66); and Mrs. Failing is her satanic accomplice.

Like her brother Herbert, Agnes slays imagination. Only "the
great world" is significant for her; and she is at enmity with Ansell's intellectual distinction, Rickie's creative expansiveness, and
Stephen's natural morality: "Actual life might seem to her so real
that she could not detect the union of shadow and adamant that
men call poetry" (164). Foreign to her is that valid sort of empiricism—a sacramental sense of the actual—which all three men at
various times reveal.

Rickie is partly justified in his disgust with Stephen's drunkenness (he fears for the desecration of Stephen's powerful organism
and for the tendency of the drunkard to resort to "second-hand"
intensities); but he also reacts too seriously, regarding the situation as a defeat of his ideals as to what other people should be.
For Mrs. Failing, Rickie is associated with "the cracked bell"
which sounds from Cadover Church. The bell is heard in the Cadbury Rings as she tells him about Stephen and again at Rickie's
funeral when, with some satisfaction, she denominates him a failure. The cracked bell signifies less his personal deficiencies and
material failure—since he does prevail in his death and after—
than his aborted career, his truncated development and influence,
his deflection from wholeness, and his defeated aspirations.

II   Rickie Elliot: Perceptive and Misguided Humanist

For the most part, values in The Longest Journey are defined,
explicitly or symbolically, through Rickie's sensibility, through his
actions, through Forster's comments upon him, and through the
views of the other characters about him. In those parts not re-

fracted through Rickie's consciousness, characters and incident ultimately impinge upon his fortunes. Perceptiveness and blindness in close conjunction make of Rickie one of the most enigmatic and complex characters in recent literature. His contradictory personality, his paradoxical ideas, his changing relationships with others, and the ironic disparities between his actual conduct and his inspiriting standards bring the book into focus and elicit from it varied chains of significance. Even at his most quixotic and weak, we retain an interest in him and perceive that he is more than the outcast and failure he judges himself to be in moments of discouraged self-appraisal at Sawston School. He gains our sympathy because it is more difficult at times to endure convention, as Rickie does, than to break with it (Stone, 193).

Both Elizabeth Bowen and Lionel Trilling, I think, have somewhat oversimplified Rickie's character. For Elizabeth Bowen (125) he is a neutral character and his personality becomes a battleground, continually fought over in turn by opposing factions. Lionel Trilling in *E. M. Forster* (1943) divides the novel dialectically between two camps, with Rickie caught passively between them and drifting into the wrong one (87). Rickie has greater force, originality, and independence, I feel, than these critics admit. Although Trilling does mention Rickie's dignity, he views him as choosing between an absolute idealism and an absolute practicality. Rather, I think, he tries to merge the two modes of existence and to live creatively in accordance with his humanistic and Christian values. He is a man, in short, of more than average insight who makes an all but disastrous mistake, a wrong marriage.

Rickie is a sensitive, perceptive individual who explores differing realms of experience and attempts to reconcile them without signal success. As Wilfred Stone in *The Cave and the Mountain* (191) and Thomson (135–39) indicate, Rickie is in part a hero of romance who is tested by ordeals in three different milieus. Yet he deserves approbation, at least in his early phases, for conscientious pursuit of truth wherever it may lead. He is drawn both to the intellectual values of Cambridge, as Ansell represents them, and to the empirical (yet mystical) realities of nature, as Stephen embodies them; he aims for a synthesis of abstract and concrete, through the agency of imagination and purely personal values, much as Tony Failing, his uncle, tried to achieve before him. In his attempts at philosophical integration, Rickie fails; his imagination lacks discipline, and he has less immediate wisdom in personal relationships than do Ansell and Stephen, for whom they are less obsessive.

But, if Rickie succumbs to the enemy of the imagination, the Philistine world of Sawston, his efforts to bridge the concrete and the transcendent and then to relate these realms of value to the larger world provide the framework upon which the most meaningful existence may be built. Rickie is deflected from attaining a vibrant synthesis, although his surviving influence enables Stephen to achieve, more fully, such a harmonizing of powers. Like a typical prophet, Rickie is sacrificed in the interest of the fuller life to be which he helps to bring about. Thomson (156) goes farther and regards Rickie's death as an intentional mutilation that is necessary for Stephen's welfare and survival. John Magnus even more pointedly gives the direction which interpretations of this novel are following when he finds its structural basis in the rituals linking Rickie and Stephen: ". . . Stephen's ablutions transform him from buffoon to husband—Rickie's sacrifice allows Stephen's marriage to take place, and thus ensures the future of England." [2]

Trilling, I feel, assumes that Rickie too willingly joins the "benighted." Rather, he struggles against malign pressures, particularly those exerted by his wife, by her brother Herbert and Sawston School, and by Emily Failing. In judging Rickie's stature, we should note that it is he who initially most trenchantly criticizes these "benighted" people. Through his own efforts, he hopes to recapture "the Holy Grail" in his work and to cure the wound wrought by esthetic and philosophical frustration. If his quest to that end is mostly futile, "his attempts to discover reality give him a certain dignity." [3]

By the end of the novel he has managed to get free of the malevolent forces at Sawston and Cadover. A certain ambiguity invests Rickie at the close, however. He defends himself eloquently against Mrs. Failing and her denial of the free life. Following his disillusion over Stephen's drunkenness and broken promise, however, he seems in death again to have denied the light and to have reverted to her views. Yet it is possible to feel that he has made his concession to his aunt—that convention is truth—with only his conscious mind and that his deeper self achieves worthy expression in laying down his life for his brother and in writing the stories, composed before and after the Sawston experience, which win for him posthumous fame and for his brother financial security. He serves the earth even while he expresses disillusionment with it to his aunt as he dies.

John Magnus in his article (209) finds in Rickie a Hermes analogue. In Classical mythology Hermes was Demeter's servant; in the novel, Rickie helps Demeter (or Mrs. Elliot) bring about Stephen's survival as a natural force, just as Hermes rescued Persephone in ancient lore from the underworld and enabled Demeter to bring back the spring. Magnus also equates Rickie with the Hermes of Praxiteles and Stephen with the child Dionysus under the god's protective care. We can carry this interpretation farther and see in Stephen himself "a divine child" like the Dionysus of the statue. It was as a child radiating light and serenity that the naked Stephen appeared long before to his uncle on the roof at Cadover house. As a divine child, he is to become the savior of his race; and he develops into a man in whom are concentered all the most durable fibers of the English people. His child in turn becomes another such harbinger of the future.

Rickie's goodwill, generosity, and human insight derive from his mother, not from his father and aunt, who are negative and evil forces. Rickie remembers his father as a man whose eyes showed unkindness, cowardice, and fear, "as if the soul looked through dirty window-panes" (32), and whose voice was suave but whip-like. The leaden frames in Mr. Elliot's flower vases, like concealed and coiled sea serpents, are emblematic of the concealed and coiled venom in his nature. The image is linked with the snake-like stream of water which intrudes into Mrs. Failing's bower as she writes the memoir of her husband. This group of images suggests a Mephistophelean element in both brother and sister. In typical moments, they express themselves through diabolical laughter. As for Mr. Elliot, he never gave himself, never did things for love, and he was, therefore, incapable of attaining the culture which most people credited him with possessing. He remained an inhumane esthete. Despite his iconoclasm, he lacked the sincerity to be truly unconventional.

In Rickie, Forster embodies many of his humanistic—and Christian—values: kindness, consideration, tact, unselfishness, and sympathy. Since these qualities are largely Christian, it is no accident that Rickie belongs to the Anglican Church. At Cambridge, Rickie's lameness does not separate him from others, since his geniality, his enthusiasm, and his good nature—qualities nurtured in him by the university—allow him to regard his defect as the minor impediment it is. Until his denial of Stephen, Rickie reflects the genius of Cambridge which educates by indirection. He hopes, moreover, that he will never be peevish or unkind; so long as he is in congenial surroundings, he never falls from his standard. The set of Rickie's moral nature, in fact, is indicated in Mrs. Failing's opinion of the half-brothers. She prefers Stephen's strength to Rickie's "blatant unselfishness"; but, in so doing, she tacitly admits Rickie's superior sensitivity and sympathy.

A sophisticated humanism should also enable us to define the complex relationship existing between beauty and ethics. Agnes maintains that Rickie is "cracked" in his enthusiasm for the pictures inside the church at Madingley Hall at Cambridge. His concern is genuine in contrast to Agnes' superficial interest; and he reveals his estheticism by maintaining that nothing beautiful is ever to be regretted. He feels, nevertheless, that beauty is only a means to the end of awareness and has little value if it does not lead to such enlargement. He admires his Uncle Tony for rejecting the arts which he loved, a "cultured paradise," for the end of securing "more decent people in the world" (200). In a quarrel with his aunt over the Church of England services at Cadover, he refuses to admit that their tawdriness reflects adversely upon Christianity. Rather, he sees that a sense of beauty whose gratification is relentlessly pursued becomes sterile and inhuman.

With the Pembrokes, practicality reigns; they serve "the great world"; they assume that their souls are thereby nourished; and they fail to obtain mastery over conflicting imperatives because they refuse to recognize the existence of values opposed to their own. Thus Agnes is robust and practical, desires only a frank good-fellowship in marriage, and discourages intimacies based on emotion. Herbert is the spokesman at Sawston for a debasing pragmatism: the use of tradition where it avails, and the use of new departures where they avail. This opportunism had been repudiated by Tony Failing, who had also been interested in the practical life but who felt that such a life could only be attained through dedication in part to ideal ends.

Like all of Forster's good humanists, Rickie attempts to reach some middle-ground between the poles of permanence and change. At his best, he acknowledges the complexities of the moral life and tries to reconcile them. Although, in his quest for certitude, he fastens with excessive tenacity upon those elements in his experience which connote the permanent, he never completely loses his flexibility. His respect for the general, the philosophical, and the universal, moreover, enriches his mind, even if it may sometimes mislead him.

In his most lucid moments, Rickie bridges in thought and conduct the gulf between the eternal and the transient. Thus he finds that "the rough sea," the incessant flux of our ordinary existence, can only be restrained by the breakwaters which humanistic culture or religion build: the culture which, embodying racial wisdom, has transcended the wasting action of time, or the religion which, powerful in spirituality, has survived the passing centuries and has as its symbols in the novel the spire of Salisbury Cathedral or the towers of St. Mary's Roman Catholic Church at Cambridge. In the modern age, the sea's disintegrative currents have not lessened; but the accretions of permanently valuable knowledge mean that the human "bubbles" on these turbulent waters break less frequently than they did formerly.

Unless the forces which lead to ceaseless change are counterweighted by others which bring a modicum of order, any sense of direction or pattern in our lives will be impossible. A genuine stability, able to assimilate or to curb pressures from without, is absent from Sawston School, despite continued recourse there to standardizing custom and convention. There, contact with ordering principle and dynamic flux are both lost: Dunwood House becomes an "unnecessary ship," lacking connection with the currents of change in the sea beneath or with the permanencies of the shore; and the sea it traverses is "frothy" and volatile, not "rough" and substantial.

That life is dynamic but has its core of permanent and ordered values is one truth implicit in the fascinating nature symbolism. In Wiltshire, streams constantly carry water to the sea while a permanent substratum of chalk underlies them; the waters erode the surfaces of the chalk formations but leave untouched their central core. Orion and the other stars vary their appearances with the seasons but always return; the Cadbury Rings last as a monument over the centuries but eminences of ground like these act as a watershed to fill the running streams and will, in thousands of years, be worn down themselves. Intellectually, Rickie understands this dichotomy but in practice he tends, as McConkey (107) and others have pointed out, to elevate some aspect of nature or some person into a rigid image and to deny the element of mutability in experience.

Nature receives ambiguous emphasis in the novel. Whereas the earth confirms the spiritual largeness of Stephen and his father Robert, these men recognize that its influence is not always beneficent; and to Rickie, responsive to its beauties, the earth seems cruel and relentless. Rickie may once again be central in his perplexity, for as Crews (60) asserts, the most searching question raised is this: "Is it possible, or even worthwhile, to uphold our private standards of value in a world that is indifferent to our existence?"

When Forster describes Rickie as suffering from "the primal curse," the "knowledge of good-and-evil," he speaks ironically; for Rickie's knowledge is also a virtue. Rickie knows there are two sides to a question; he often sees the other side to his immediate detriment. Comprehension of moral complexity characterizes subtly intelligent people like Rickie, who are in contrast with the unimaginative, falsely simplifying Pembrokes. Those who understand most things suffer most; the sensitive suffer for their sensitivity, as does Rickie in this novel. If full knowledge sometimes immobilizes him for positive action, it enables him to probe deeply into life so long as he is true to his best impulses. It is his tragedy that in practice his mind grows less supple, that at Sawston he becomes "the limpet" to Herbert's "whelk," and that he loses his sense of life as "good-and-evil" when he condones the absolutist standards of Sawston.

III   Structure in The Longest Journey: *The Role of Persons and Places*

The tripartite structure emphasizes the crucial importance for Rickie of places and the people who inhabit them. The novel consists of three symphony-like movements, "Cambridge," "Sawston," and "Wiltshire"; and this pattern was to be followed in both *Howards End* and *A Passage to India*. Forster also uses more intricately than in *Where Angels Fear to Tread* and *A Room with a View* the repeated image with variations to secure an incremental symbolic effect. In so doing, he heralds his practice in his last two novels. Examples of such recurring motifs are the following: Ansell's exercise of putting squares into constantly diminishing circles; flowing streams; chalk; Orion; Demeter; the Cadbury Rings; Salisbury Cathedral spire; Agnes as Medusa; the cow and its "reality"; Mrs. Elliot's voice from the dead; the railroad level-crossing and the bridge eventually built there; the references to Wagner in connection with Agnes and with the bridge and water motifs; flame and fire; and the Madingley Dell. I cannot analyze fully all these recurring image clusters, although I refer to many of them incidentally.

Ansell is Forster's spokesman at many points, and he is sympathetically presented, especially in "Cambridge." He is devoted to the life of the intellect but is often able to see more truthfully the plain facts of existence than Rickie does. Despite his perception of the primacy of the affections, he is, in practice, often too exclusive and superior in his views of other people; and his histrionic instincts override a tactful exercise of sympathy, when, for example, he enjoys exposing Rickie's rejection of Stephen to the assembled personnel of Dunwood House. As Rickie sees, Ansell is better at discussing love and death in the abstract than at analyzing lovers and dying men. He is not yet the true heir of the ancients, but is acquiring by the end of the book fuller understanding of Classical virtues and of ancient civilization with the knowledge imparted by Stephen and by the essays of Tony Failing. At the British Museum he does not yet penetrate to the more reticent—or the deeper—values of humanity: the forces of earth symbolized by the Cnidian Demeter, the transmuting power of parental love that informs the temple of Ephesian Artemis, and the infinite serenities implicit in the Parthenon friezes. At this point, only the pathos of the vanished civilization registers with him, not the consecrating power to be found in the vital traditions of the Greeks.

I agree with Crews (62) when he says that Ansell's notion of the good is "unclouded" since "he feels no need to seek confirmation for it in the outside world." But I do not regard this attitude as entirely positive. It is just possible that Ansell fails to "connect" the varieties of experience. Rickie is less steady than Ansell, but he is also subjected to pressures when he leaves the Cambridge community that are unknown to his friend.

The second movement, "Sawston," dramatizes the corrupting influence of Philistine England upon Rickie when, in order to marry Agnes, he consents to be a master at her brother's school. As its title would indicate, "Wiltshire," the third movement, emphasizes what had only been previously hinted, the redemptive influence of earth. Appropriately, the man who establishes the closest contact with the earth, Stephen's father Robert, figures for the first time; and we are taken to the past and the circumstances of his elopement with Mrs. Elliot. Again, as in the first movements of the novel, events involving Stephen prove decisive for Rickie. The flame boat episode in Chapter 23 is climactic in its assertion of the newfound unity between the brothers, whereas in Chapter 24 Stephen's broken promise to Rickie to desist from drinking separates them.

Through Stephen, the powers of earth over the spirit are forcibly asserted. Full rapport with the energies of nature implants in him an elemental wisdom which enables him to discern pretentiousness of all kinds. In spite of his lack of education, he has the intuitive insight of Forster's archetypal characters. Accordingly, in the epilogue he deflates Herbert Pembroke who, Stephen feels, has always been bound by conventions and the desire to "tidy" out of existence those who do not conform to them. Later, when Stephen sleeps out at night with his child, he ritualistically confirms his oneness with the earth. Instinctively identifying himself with the forces of continuity cherished by Forster, he knows that he has created life and that over the centuries men with his passions and thoughts will triumph in England.

Tony Failing had said there is no such person as a Londoner: he is only a man fallen from the life-giving forces to be found in rural traditions. As a sign of his increased wisdom, Rickie learns that towns are "excrescences" in which men lead purposeless lives. When the brothers return to Cadover, they are aware that the power of earth grows stronger as they leave Salisbury behind. The only ornament in Stephen's room at Cadover, a framed picture of the Demeter of Cnidus, indicates his affinity with this goddess of earth. The fact that the picture sways from a cord in the middle of his attic may signify that Demeter's influence over him is dynamic rather than static. In the epilogue, the Demeter of Cnidus is also linked with Rickie, who in his way is also a spiritual scion of the Greeks. As the last rays of the sun illuminate "the immortal features and the shattered knees" of the goddess in Stephen's new home, we recall not only Rickie at his death when the train at the level crossing had run over his legs but Stephen at the ford when the roseate glow from the flame boat lights his face. The Demeter, moreover, attracts Stephen's little girl, who says goodbye to the "stone lady" as she goes out with her father to sleep on the downs. The Demeter is thus a stone figure who infuses life; paradoxically, the flesh-and-blood Agnes becomes the stony "Medusa in Arcady" who infuses death.

The relationship of the individual to Greek and Roman civilization indicates his relative worth. Rickie's bonds with Greece and Rome are intellectual; Stephen's are physical. Upon occasion, their attitudes are almost identical; and the tragedy of their being kept apart by Mrs. Failing's manipulation of their situation is thereby intensified. Early in the novel, Rickie responds to the poetry of the heavens whose stars have been named by the Greeks; Stephen's own wonder at the night is never fully exhausted, and its stars glow brightly as he speculates at the end of the novel on his future. With his mind, Rickie poetically elaborates his experience and places meaningful veils of gods and goddesses between himself and reality; with his body, Stephen reacts directly to outside forces, his passion for drink, for example, being met with Dionysian directness.

The boys complement each other. With the help of nature, they might indeed have been made whole in each other's presence; and Demeter, Stephen's patron goddess, would have rejoiced in the fraternal union. The very names of the horses they ride over the downs to Salisbury indicate their differing destinies as well as their native Classical sympathies. Stephen, who will persist through his progeny, rides Aeneas, whose namesake had been the founder of a new kingdom. Rickie, an admirable youth deflected from his true destiny by an unfortunate love affair, rides Dido, whose namesake had also met a tragic end through mistaken perceptions of her loved one's nature and purposes.

The phrase from the *Georgics*, "O Pan, keeper of sheep," establishes Tony Failing and Rickie as mental heirs of the ancients; Stephen, as pagan in spirit. When Stephen as a boy was stampeded by sheep, Mr. Failing had repeated the phrase as he succored him; at school, Stephen is later punished for comically mistranslating the words, as if to demonstrate that literature itself is of subsidiary worth for one who has "been back somewhere— back to some table of the gods" (245) and been initiated, once **for**

all, into the company of immortals. Rickie opens his teaching at
Sawston with these Virgilian lines; their beauty is to him overwhelming, but he gets no response from the philistine-minded
boys and soon gives up the task of stirring them spiritually.

As a primal force and mythic presence, Stephen is compelling.
Whether he is capacious enough even as an archetypal figure to
absorb the forces of the intellect, man, nature, and imagination
(represented by Ansell, Tony Failing, Mrs. Elliot, and Rickie)
represents the crux of the novel. As brute and natural man, he
convinces; but it is doubtful that he embodies fully the Classical
and intellectual values. George H. Thomson has convinced me that
Stephen is an archetypal hero by virtue of his native force and
insight, and that he supplants, as the focal center of interest, the
failed hero, Rickie Elliot. And yet I think that the majority of
critics[4] are right in judging Stephen as not quite adequate to
Forster's abstract conception of him.

When Angus Wilson, in a recent talk with Forster, said he
"thought most highly of *The Longest Journey* of all his novels,"
Forster enthusiastically agreed. With Forster we can recognize
this novel, despite its flaws, as a work of major significance for its
thematic complexity, its psychological subtlety, its human sympathy, and its suggestive artistry.

CHAPTER 4

"Glimpses of the Diviner Wheels": Howards End

I *Division and Reconciliation: Structure and Rhythm in* Howards End

*H*OWARDS *End* is the first of Forster's two main achievements as a novelist. Although the book lacks the full control and maturity of *A Passage to India,* it is a more zestful and engaging performance. Its strength derives from characters who compel our interest and from the subtlety of its organization. F. R. Leavis, Walter Allen in "Reassessments—*Howards End,*" and other earlier critics tended to underscore its flaws; but most recent commentators, such as Malcolm Bradbury, have stressed the scope and challenge of a book[1] written so directly "about the circumstances in which the moral life, which is also the full life of the imagination, can be led in society, about the compromises which it must effect with itself if it is to do so, and about the moral and imaginative value of making certain such compromises." In the last analysis, *Howards End* may be regarded highly for its fusion of character and situation with idea; for the skill evinced in bringing all segments of the British middle class to bear upon each other; for the interweaving of social comedy with serious, often tragic, situations; for the connotative richness of its symbols; and for the freshness, wit, beauty, and polish of its style.

At its most explicit, the novel is concerned with the connections existing between two segments of the English middle class: the Schlegels and the Wilcoxes. The Schlegel sisters are artistically inclined women of leisure, they possess humane sympathies, they espouse Forster's humanistic values, they appreciate a life-giving culture, and they recognize the graces of the spirit. Opposed to them are the practical, materialistic, enterprising, and knowledgeable Wilcoxes, who are seen as typical of the commercial class that has made England strong and wealthy. As Crews observes (106), the two families complement each other: Henry

Wilcox, the empire builder, needs "the civilizing force of liberalism"; and the Schlegels, advocates of liberalism, need Henry Wilcox' political and economic power.

Ruth Wilcox is an outsider in the midst of her extrovert family; but she softens the rough edges of her husband and children and earns their respect, even if they can never understand her. Though she derives from yeoman ancestry and though she knows by instinct the details of the lives of all in her family, still she and daily life are "out of focus." She arrives at her conclusions through intuition rather than through reason; she represents those intangible values of the spirit opposed to the material standards of her family. She embodies, moreover, the qualities associated with tradition and the earth which make for renewal.

Although she is the source of life in others, she has attained a resignation not far from indifference. She only becomes animated when she is at Howards End, her Hertfordshire house and ancestral home, or when she discusses it. Otherwise, especially in London, she reveals a fatigue and a cynicism that anticipate Mrs. Moore's nihilism in *A Passage to India*: "Mrs. Wilcox's voice, though sweet and compelling, had little range of expression. It suggested that pictures, concerts, and people are all of small and equal value" (70).

In the first pages, Ruth Wilcox at Howards End separates the incompatible Helen Schlegel and Paul Wilcox. Later, in London, she becomes the close friend of Margaret Schlegel and brings the families together. After her sudden death, the widower Henry falls in love with Margaret, possibly because she has so many of Ruth's attributes. In the course of the novel, Henry and Margaret weather some differences to become devoted husband and wife.

Considerably before Henry becomes romantically involved with Margaret, he had headed a family council that decided to set aside the last wish of wife and mother: to bequeath Howards End to Margaret. The fact that Ruth wills her most cherished possession to Margaret indicates that in her friend Ruth has found a spiritual heir. The act of burning the will signifies that the Wilcoxes are estranged from Ruth's values and are not receptive either to Margaret's similar influence. But Margaret is not yet mature enough to become Ruth's successor. After the Wilcoxes have been subdued by tragedy and Margaret has been mellowed by her disturbing relationships with Henry and Helen, it is time for her to claim, by sheer spiritual authority, her inheritance. At the close of the novel, when Henry transfers the house to her and she learns for the first time about the will, she is ready to assume her symbolic role as tutelary priestess at Howards End to succeed Ruth. During the main part of the novel, Howards End is deserted since Ruth dies early in the action and she alone of her family feels affection for the place.

The influence of Ruth Wilcox, before her death and after, brings the Schlegels and Wilcoxes to a new understanding. The influence of Leonard Bast, a clerk with intellectual pretensions whom the Schlegels first meet at a concert, divides the families. The Schlegels adopt him as protégé; and they act on Henry's advice, counseling him to change his job. He does so; but, because of fluctuations in the business world, he is ruined. Helen champions the outcast; and because she holds Henry responsible, she and the Basts storm into the opulent wedding of his daughter, Evie, at Oniton Grange in Shropshire. She demands that Henry make reparation to Leonard. The situation is complicated beyond Margaret's power to do anything for Leonard when she—and we as readers—learn the full truth. Leonard's wife, Jacky, recognizes Henry as a former lover of hers in Cyprus during his marriage to Ruth. Margaret, nevertheless, decides to keep to her engagement; but in doing so, she recognizes that she can have no more to do with the Basts.

Helen, in revulsion against Henry's hostility and Margaret's indifference and in an excess of pity for Leonard, gives herself to him. The result is a pregnancy which Helen conceals by deserting both lover and sister and retreating to the Continent. Eight months later, when Helen is lured to Howards End through Margaret's anxiety and Henry's craft, Margaret learns the truth. Henry's lack of sympathy for one who has transgressed, even as he has, virtually wrecks his marriage. Because he refuses to allow her to stay with Helen for one night at Howards End and because he insists on treating Helen as fallen, Margaret decides to go to Germany with her sister to be with her during childbirth and later.

Leonard in death and Ruth Wilcox in spirit finally counter at Howards End the forces making for division between the Schlegels and the Wilcoxes. When Leonard comes to Margaret to confess his adultery with Helen, he is accosted as a blackguard by

the robust and unimaginative Charles Wilcox, who had learned
the name of Helen's "seducer" from her brother, Tibby. Lacking
vitality, strength, and assertiveness, Leonard dies after Charles
beats him. Charles is convicted of manslaughter, although it is
probable that Leonard died from natural causes. Henry, who is
broken by his son's imprisonment, begs Margaret to reconsider
her decision to leave him. She decides that all she can do is to
bring the two people who most need her help, Helen and Henry,
to Howards End to recover.

The concluding sequence, set at Howards End fourteen months
after Leonard's death, has been much criticized. We must agree
that, all things considered, the spectacle of a subdued Henry and
a restored Helen with her healthy child, all dwelling at Howards
End under Margaret's aegis, hardly represents an adequate resolution for the complex issues and relationships explored. There is
point, for example, to Samuel Hynes' contention in "Forster at
Eighty-Five" (637) that the divisive elements are too strong to be
overcome and that the epigraph to the novel might better be "If
only we could connect" instead of "Only connect." If this scene is
not in all respects persuasive, it is nevertheless symbolically more
successful than some critics have been willing to grant. On the
realistic plane, a submissive Henry Wilcox does violence to his
role in England's destiny, which Forster had intellectually fixed
for him; Leonard Bast's death may be regarded as fortuitous; and
Charles' imprisonment as arbitrary.

Yet we can, I think, follow the lead of John Edward Hardy in
Man in the Modern Novel (46–50), who sees the concluding
chapter as a fertility ritual over which the absent spirit of Ruth
Wilcox presides and as a victory for the transcendent powers
which she had embodied throughout. The energies of nature with
which she is identified expose both the sterile progressivism of the
Wilcoxes and the abstract personalism of the Schlegels. Responsive always to spiritual modes of apprehension, however, the
Schlegels quickly respond to the healing influence of house, field,
tree, and vine at Howards End; for Ruth Wilcox has not educated
their souls in vain. In one sense, Howards End is indeed the symbol
of England, especially of the best traditions that she stands for, as
Trilling maintains (118). In another sense, Hilton Station, with its
indeterminate quality suggesting both an industrial and pastoral
culture, is a more precise microcosm of present-day England. Sta-

tion and countryside alike are poised between these two modes of existence. Which one will survive, only the future can tell.

The triumph of Howards End and the Schlegel values is by no means assured, as London and the Wilcox values creep always closer to a house which seems to assume the aspect of an increasingly beleaguered fortress. The Schlegels may again at any time be called upon to defend themselves and their heritage. Far from being sentimentalized as some think, I find the concluding sequence suffused with a sympathetic irony. Helen's child only incidentally takes part in a realistic pastoral idyll. He is, in effect, a Blakean child, innocent perhaps but apocalyptic in his innocence, a divine child. He serves the same purpose as Gino's baby, who is killed, in *Where Angels Fear to Tread;* as the boy Stephen on the roof of Cadover house in *The Longest Journey;* as Stephen's child in that novel; and as the unborn child of Fielding and Stella in *A Passage to India.*

Ruth Wilcox continually hints at transcendent values with which all the characters must come to terms, and she becomes for Thomson and others an "archetypal" character by virtue of her visionary sensitivity. If we believe Margaret after her reunion with Helen, all people in the novel have their separate existences only as parts of Ruth's mind. In the last chapter Forster refers to Margaret as "Mrs. Wilcox" for the first time, as if to indicate that she has now assumed Ruth Wilcox' role as mediator and peacemaker. Helen assumes Mrs. Wilcox' other role, that of mother. And Margaret has been able to come to terms with the Wilcox clan, who begin to pay her the begrudging respect that Ruth Wilcox had earned before her.

Margaret's comment to Henry that "nothing has been done wrong" (342) is perhaps too sweeping; but it suggests that serenity has been won through suffering, that divisions between the characters have been healed, that "the rainbow bridge" of abiding love has indeed been fashioned. As in romance, the characters are tested; all except Leonard survive their ordeals. We might grant that the concluding sequence lacks some of the spiritual expansiveness that accompanies genuine tragedy; yet the novel as a whole often attains these larger dimensions.

As in *The Longest Journey* and *A Passage to India,* we can detect a three-part movement in this novel, even if Forster did not name the units. Like these other novels, *Howards End* moves for-

ward in sweeping movements of related incidents and depends
for unity on parallel scenes and on a repetition of incidents,
themes, and symbolic images. The novel thereby gains clarity of
intellectual line and intricacy of design.

The first chapter dramatizes the theme of unity and separation
between the Schlegels and the Wilcoxes. First, Helen's letter to
Margaret announces her engagement to Paul; then her telegram
announces the break between them. The next eleven chapters
trace the rebuilding of the relationship between the Schlegels and
the Wilcoxes. This movement is brought to an end with Ruth's
sudden death and her burial in Hertfordshire, the destruction of
Ruth's will by her family which acts as a "committee," and Margaret's sense of loss and her accession of wisdom as a result of her
friend's passing.

For Ruth Wilcox suggests to Margaret that the spirit is immortal if the body is not, that only when one is dead does the spirit
assume full authority. Margaret sees that Ruth Wilcox in death
escapes "registration" and that her friend's remains are truly dust
—not in the sense that she is to be soon forgotten but in the sense
that she endures in so many intangible ways. The novel instructs
us that, despite the existence of physical death, the force of life
itself is immortal: in Hilton churchyard where Ruth has just been
buried, a laborer emblematically plucks one of Margaret's chry-
santhemums for his sweetheart, and at the end of the novel the
dead Leonard with the live narcissi in his hand is to be survived by
a son. From Ruth Wilcox, Margaret learns that hope is certain
"this side of the grave" and that "truer relationships" are possible.
Later, when Margaret learns to love Howards End, she absorbs
wisdom from the house and the countryside just as Ruth had done
before her.

The second movement of the novel stretches from Chapter 13,
which picks up the Schlegels and the Basts two years after the
funeral, to Chapter 30, which features Helen's interview with her
brother Tibby at Oxford following the disastrous expedition to
Oniton Grange with the Basts. This part of the novel continues
with the masterly presentation of Henry Wilcox' courtship of
Margaret, her reasoned decision to marry him, and the threat to
their relationship by the events at Oniton when Henry's past life
with Jacky Bast comes to light.

The last movement of the novel analyzes Margaret's marriage

and her estrangement from Helen. The pattern of this "movement" of chapters follows that in the second "movement." Again, the relationship between Margaret and Henry attains firmness; and the combined influence of Helen and Leonard challenges it. Although in the preceding section Margaret had followed sexual instinct and remained loyal to Henry, she now chooses her sister as Howards End itself seems to suggest that she should. The sanctities of long standing between herself and Helen, intensified by the presence of the Schlegel furniture in the old house, motivate her after Henry proves obdurate about Helen. Margaret's rejection of her husband is the first climax of this third section; the second is the death of Leonard, with the consequent undermining of Henry's confidence and strength. Henry's loss of nerve leads, in turn, to Margaret's muted triumph in the concluding chapter.

The novel is unified, in large part, by the presence of repeated images which attain symbolic intonations. Examples are the house at Howards End, the wych-elm tree with concealed pig's teeth in its bark and the vine at Howards End, the Wilcox motor car, the Wilcox regimen of "telegrams and anger," the "goblin footfall" present in the Beethoven Fifth Symphony, the "abyss" close to the edge of which dwell the Basts, the grayness of London as opposed to the variegated life of the country, the hay associated with Mrs. Wilcox and later with Margaret, and the books, the bookcase, and the Schlegel sword (these latter are stored at Howards End after Margaret's marriage to Henry and unpacked by Miss Avery, Ruth Wilcox' friend and constituent). Symbolism in *Howards End* is so complex that I can only discuss it incidentally.

George H. Thomson and William H. Rueckert in *Kenneth Burke and the Drama of Human Relations* (1963) demonstrate the lengths to which informed discussion of the symbolism of this novel can take us. Rueckert, who studies *Howards End* in light of Burke's terminology, demonstrates the "dramatistic" aspect or the far-reaching implications of one of the chief symbols, the wych-elm, in as many pages as I have for my entire discussion. The presence of these symbols illustrates the "easy rhythm" which Forster mentions in *Aspects of the Novel,* as one means by which an author can unify a novel. Such a rhythm is "easy" in the sense that author and reader can with some precision isolate the elements that comprise it.

Howards End also illustrates a more elusive, "difficult" rhythm in the images of flux and flow that are integral to its texture and deeper meaning. James McConkey brilliantly analyzes this range of imagery (107–17). He finds two contrasting kinds of movement; undirected and disintegrative movement, reflected through the meaningless activity of the city and the violent motion of the Wilcox motor car; and ordered change, reflected through the motions of nature, without which life would perish through inanition. The merging of the seasons into one another and the flow of the tides and rivers embody this regulated mobility basic to the processes of nature and their fruition.

Such "rhythms" elicit, as do similar patterns in *A Passage to India*, a sense that time stands still even as we know that it passes, that eternity lurks behind the transient shows of life, that the currents of life move inevitably to a settled calm even as they leave behind the chaotic present. Change and movement toward some ordered end—such is also the direction of Margaret's inner existence. But she knows that her aspirations for the eternal have, in the world of the here and now, only limited possibilities of being realized.

II "A More Inward Light": Forster's Subtle Dialectic

Although the novel works in the direction of a rapprochement between the Schlegels and the Wilcoxes, a contrary movement is discernible. Critics such as Cyrus Hoy and James Hall are right in noting that Margaret must not so much learn to reconcile her standards to those of the Wilcoxes as to appraise the Wilcoxes for what they are—to see critically their materialism, hypocrisy, brutality, and spiritual emptiness. The primacy of the inner life is again asserted at the novel's end, but the sisters have lost their complacency about it. "The goblin footfall" of the third movement of the Fifth Symphony still threatens to negate a potential heroism, including Margaret's own "heroic" struggle to span the segments of the middle class; and the "abyss" on whose edge the Basts of Edwardian England precariously live dispels an easy optimism. The sisters try to alleviate squalor and injustice but realize that their efforts may not amount to much.

Yet, if the Wilcox values violate much of what the Schlegels stand for, the sisters have achieved through them a new stability. The Wilcoxes have at least preserved Howards End from destruction and have brought the Schlegels there. Yet what the Wilcoxes predominantly represent is "the inner darkness in high places that comes with a commercial age" (331); and their sphere of activity is the city whose aspect, especially in the fog, is "Satanic" and suggests "a darkening of the spirit which fell back on itself, to find a more grievous darkness within" (84).

The difference between the families is that existing between two approaches to experience. A full appreciation of the seen or the natural, such as the Wilcoxes reveal, will lead to a steady comprehension of life; but an informed sensitivity to the unseen or the immaterial, such as the Schlegels reveal, will lead to a perception of life in its wholeness. Henry sees life steadily; Margaret sees it whole. Wholeness, Forster thus implies, is more to be valued since it will prevent the one-sidedness which often marks the man of affairs and causes Margaret to break with Henry.

The dialectic, as we have seen, brings together inner and outer, the inner world of intellect and culture and the external world of physical and commercial activity. The schematic quality of the book, however, has been overemphasized, largely because earlier critics concentrated on the relationships between the Schlegels and the Wilcoxes. More recently, critics have emphasized the supple nature of the dialectic which is complex enough to allow for several movements or "connections" to be made. Margaret, of course, connects the prose with the passion of life through the understanding, sympathy, and imagination she reveals in the relationship with Henry Wilcox; but she manifests these same qualities, perhaps more spontaneously, in establishing firmer understandings with Helen and with the spirit of Ruth Wilcox.

Margaret is led by love to expect too much from Henry; Helen is led by her passion for truth to anticipate too much from her sister. From Margaret's partial success in closing the distance between the Schlegels and the Wilcoxes, Helen learns that her conception of truth had been too constricted and her championship of the Basts too impulsive. Her idealism, moreover, had been driven into a sexual emotion so absolute that it ruined Leonard more completely than Henry Wilcox could ever have done. At this point, Helen is incensed at Henry's having destroyed Leonard Bast twice. Blinded by the passions of the moment, she cannot judge the effects of her own actions; the result is that she ruins him a third time, despite her most generous motives.

The sisters learn, Helen especially, that the credo of personal relationships is difficult to apply in the circumstances of actual life; they must learn that a belief, no matter how noble, is still a formula until the imagination makes of it a viable reality. Thus both sisters fail Leonard Bast since they regard him more as a representative of a lower social class than as a human being important in his own right. They patronize him insufferably: "Mr. Bast! I and my sister have talked you over. We wanted to help you; we also supposed you might help us . . ." (143); "We want to show him how he may get upsides with life" (145). But Margaret's refusal to help Leonard at Oniton reveals that she values him as an individual with his own dignity; for Helen, he is a *casus belli* in her opposition to the Wilcoxes.

Margaret learns from Helen, moreover, that she has been too hopeful and credulous with respect to the Wilcoxes. Anxious to give them credit for what they have done, she underestimates Henry's obtuseness and overestimates his ability to connect with people and with values opposite to his own. At the end she sees her husband realistically and no longer tries to mitigate his faults. She accepts him for what he is, without losing her affection for him. The logic of the novel may insist that Margaret and Henry have found a durable relationship; Forster's own sympathies, as James Hall in "Forster's Family Reunions" (14) points out, force us to realize that the relationship between Helen and Margaret has become the imperishable one. The sisters reassert their humanistic values and achieve a greater solidarity than do Henry and Margaret. They tacitly acknowledge a partial failure in their attempts to connect with people outside their own sphere, as with Henry Wilcox and Leonard Bast.

Still, Margaret's connection with Ruth Wilcox is possibly more important than that with Helen; for through Ruth's example, Margaret is able to connect the intellectual world of Wickham Place and the material world of the Wilcoxes with the world of intangible and transcendent values, particularly as they find expression in Howards End house, the traditions that it represents, and the countryside that surrounds it. At the beginning, Margaret is deficient in tact, understanding, and wisdom; and she comes off less well than Ruth Wilcox in their initial London encounters.

Margaret has qualities lacking in Ruth, notably a sense for social realities and an appreciation of intellect. Perhaps neither Margaret nor Ruth Wilcox is complete at their first meeting. But

Ruth is more assured since her values are based upon the intuitions of the heart rather than upon the generalizations of the mind. In the course of the novel, Margaret becomes more like Ruth Wilcox, achieves much of her native insight, and acquires much of her sensitivity to the ineffable without losing her humanist's respect for the reason. Through Ruth, Margaret develops a knowledge of what should be done in the crises of family life, though Ruth herself had retreated too far from the outer world to make her ideas effective in it. Yet the unmellowed intellect, revealed in Margaret's London friends and sometimes in Margaret herself, is less able to cope with facts than Ruth's instinctive wisdom is.

When Margaret has grown more sensitive to the realities represented by Ruth Wilcox and has been able to cultivate those "periods of quiet necessary for full growth," she achieves a more dynamic reconciliation between the earthly and the transcendent than Ruth Wilcox had. As Ruth Wilcox had been, Margaret becomes a Demeter-figure, attaining at moments intuitions into the divine, since she, too, like Forster's version of Demeter, is not only a sibylline presence but has also transcended sex to achieve identity with a reality beyond the personal.[2] Some critics feel that Margaret loses individuality when she grows more like Ruth Wilcox, some feel that she gains in stature the nearer she approaches the ideals represented by Ruth, but all agree that there is change.[3] It is Margaret's "profound vivacity" which distinguishes her from Ruth. Sometimes this quality leads to a commitment deeper than any shown by Ruth; sometimes, to a superficiality absent from her. On this question of Margaret's growth I agree with the judgment that it is her function to develop, to illustrate the principle of "becoming," instead of remaining quiescent "at the apex of being," as Ruth Wilcox always seems to do.[4]

Margaret has to attain "proportion" by excursions toward, and withdrawals from, the extremes of experience; she can accept neither the visionary idealism of Helen without critical scrutiny nor the unmitigated pragmatism of the Wilcoxes. In the central section, as Thomson (177) points out, Helen loses her ability to connect and is unable, therefore, to dominate her experience. But Margaret defines the self and its attributes with a firmer sense of reality and with a discriminating intelligence often in abeyance in both Helen and the Wilcoxes, absent in part even from Ruth Wilcox. More than Helen, certainly, Margaret "does understand herself, she has some rudimentary control over her own growth" (279).

Forster prizes throughout the values of both Margaret and Ruth Wilcox. Through Margaret, Forster advocates the civilized life of proportion; her intellectuality will be seasoned through increased affinity with her friend's spiritual sensitivity. Ruth's selfless, spontaneous qualities have absolute worth also; and what she stands for gains authority because Margaret intellectually values her friend's instinctive insights. Foreign to both women are the self-regarding subjectivity of Helen, the self-regarding objectivity of Paul and Charles Wilcox, the civilized artifice of Tibby Schlegel, and the unreflective worldliness of Henry Wilcox.

Margaret Schlegel ultimately does more than Ruth Wilcox to relate the strength of the spirit to mundane reality. Margaret would prevent the inner life from becoming solipsistic by projecting it outward to the everyday world, from which Ruth withdraws in tacit protest against its triviality. Margaret might also be criticizing Ruth Wilcox when she judges as inadequate Tibby's retreat from purposeful endeavor to a contemplative existence which he describes as "civilization without activity." A middle course between a withdrawn state of contemplation, represented by Ruth Wilcox, and an excessive commitment either to a social cause or to a mystical reality, represented by Helen Schlegel, is indispensable for regulating our inner experiences. The disinterested life of the spirit must be tested, in short, by an interested life in the tangible world.

After World War I Forster did not relinquish entirely his earlier premise. He has continued to regard "the unseen," the immaterial, and the sempiternal as no more indispensable for apprehending the meaning of existence than are the concretions of experience. Yet the complications of the life within are often lost through being elusive, they are not always apparent to those who are afraid to pass beyond an outer regime of "telegrams and anger," and they are too readily discounted in a society which emphasizes secular advantages more than the affections. The mystical is not more important than the empiric but is more likely to be overlooked. Since the English are distrustful of the metaphysical, Ruth Wilcox fears for her material-minded progeny; and she had especially desired for Charles as a child "a more inward light." Margaret also wishes to give to her husband something more than the stolid traditions which the English ordinarily bring to one another: "this blend of Sunday church and fox-hunting."

III *Technique and Character Portrayal in* Howards End

The best discussion of Forster's technique in *Howards End* is Malcolm Bradbury's. He sums up what many commentators have felt: that this novel is a remarkable fusion of social realism and of poetic symbolism, its meaning at once related to men as they are and to the aspirations of those who are most gifted and perceptive. For the juxtaposing of these two approaches to reality enables Forster to comment incisively upon the dualities of our experience. The interplay of the comic and poetic modes, then, animates the book:

> By throwing them into contrast, a mass of intellectual, moral, philosophical and social questions are raised; a dialectic is created in which the national contrasts with the international, the seen with the unseen, the practical with the romantic, the prose with the poetry and the passion; and the expectation that the book raises from its early pages is of conflict and possible synthesis, in which the terms of the dialectic are extended and laid bare. ("E. M. Forster's *Howards End*," 232)

As to social comedy, Forster never falters. It is the most perfectly achieved aspect of the novel, but the incisive style and the genuine beauty of many scenes haunt the memory longest. The sequences that include Aunt Julie's imbroglio with the Wilcoxes on Helen's behalf, Margaret's discussion with an uninterested Tibby about his future, the Wilcoxes' committee-like manner and actions concerning Ruth's bequest, the exaggerated protectiveness of Henry Wilcox and his friends for the women they bring down from London to Shropshire for Evie's wedding, the good-natured ineptitude of Dolly Wilcox whenever she confronts Henry Wilcox or her husband Charles, the first steps in the courtship between Margaret and Henry at Simpson's restaurant in London, and the distraught Helen Schlegel's conference with a placid Tibby in his Oxford rooms after the Oniton affair—all reveal Forster's expertise in the comic mode. Comedy modulates into sardonic satire

when Charles voices his contempt for the "artistic beastliness" of
the Schlegels, when he feels at Oniton Grange that Margaret
might be about to tempt him sexually, when Margaret's sophisticated friends fail to understand Ruth Wilcox at the London
luncheon, and when Aunt Julie and her German relative Frieda
Mosebach chauvinistically extol the merits of their separate countries.

The primary themes emerge from the interactions of the characters, not only as they affect one another as social beings but as
they confront in their relationships the ultimate realities of existence. In this mixture of social comedy and poetic symbolism, Forster reveals a primary indebtedness to George Meredith. Forster's
novels are less massive than Meredith's, however, and are more
tightly controlled as artistic structures. A fusion of social comedy
and poetry enables both novelists to achieve unique effects: the
comedy gives distance to the poetry which provides, in its turn, a
receding and dissolving frame for the humorous sequences.

Although Forster reveals his standards directly or by implication through all his characters, Margaret Schlegel is his chief assim-
ilative and questing intelligence. At times, as she matures, she
achieves those wider perspectives and depths of insight that betoken vision. She is, in fact, the ardent advocate of Forster's humanistic values with their emphasis on individuality, self-fulfill-
ment, personal relationships, imaginative sensitivity, sympathy
and compassion, knowledge and understanding, and a vital culture.

For most readers, Margaret is a sympathetic character. At
points, she is a bit too assured of her values (the Wilcoxes "were
deficient where she excelled") or too complacent about her own
existence ("culture had worked in her own case"); she may strike
us as a bit overbearing toward the Wilcoxes; and she is sometimes
embarrassingly direct in proclaiming her ideas. Forster is so
closely identified with her, both as protagonist and as spokesman,
that the distance between himself and Margaret is too narrow for
her always to be dramatically effective in enunciating her ideas.
Still, his humanistic gospel is attractive enough so that Margaret is
not reduced appreciably as a character when she sets forth ideas.
For the most part, too, she embodies Forster's views instead of
merely stating them. Margaret believes in being true to her own
standards and in applying them, with varying degrees of success,

to the people and the crises she encounters in her somewhat refractory existence.

Ruth Wilcox acts as a brooding presence and pervades the
novel the more completely by virtue of her death early in the
action. At times she does suggest the "greatness" which Forster
imputes to her. She is believable as a natural aristocrat and as one
who illustrates "the deeply moral quality of taste, which the intellect is powerless by itself to attain." [5] But she is so ineffectual as a
person that she fails to be compelling as a superhuman force.[6]
Perhaps because she is so real as a crotchety woman, she fails to
persuade on a more philosophical plane. As a presiding genius
and guardian figure, she does not quite overspread the novel. She
is, in fact, sometimes static and two-dimensional in contrast with
Mrs. Moore, the more fully envisioned guardian presence in *A
Passage to India*.

Forster is successful with Helen Schlegel, a girl who somewhat
stridently seeks those spiritual heights where Ruth Wilcox dwells
serenely by instinct. She disregards, moreover, the truth that the
immaterial must reveal itself through the material. This lesson she
learns at Howards End late in the novel when she finds that
house, tree, and furniture give her a surer basis than intellectual
discussion for a renewed relationship with Margaret.

Helen, who broods on the unseen, lacks the control which mystical experience often confers; rather, she is motivated by instinct
and passion; and, for a lover of the absolute, she is highly sexed.
Though she is critical of those who fail in their responsibilities, she
is appalled by the responsibilities which originate in her own
yielding to passion. As for Leonard, Helen finds that cash pay-
ment is easier than sustaining a difficult relationship.

The affair with Leonard has often been considered unreal,[7] and
there may be something to be said for the view that Helen as an
Edwardian lady would not have given herself to him. Such a
view, I think, minimizes the element of passion in Helen, her
great resentment against the Wilcoxes, and the "tense, wounding
excitement" suffusing her conduct at Oniton. Forster was also
demonstrating in Helen's sexual lapse that bodily passion is often
a concomitant of strong intellectual commitment. Her charm, cor-
diality, and generosity are genuine; and her defects are the easily
forgiven ones which derive from excessive feeling, from the warm
subjectivity of the romantic temperament. Even while she is preg-

nant with an illegitimate child, she suggests the seraphic quality of a madonna as the vine at Howards End frames her head and shoulders while the sun "glorifies" her hair.

Some central insights in the novel are also Helen's. She responds most spontaneously to Beethoven's Fifth Symphony and thereby dramatizes some of Forster's central values. She hears in the music the eternal conflict between human aspiration and the "goblin footfalls" of evil which challenge heroism but also provide it with its excuse for being. Forster, like Beethoven and Helen, hears the goblin footfalls in the distance and knows that any triumph can only be muted and short-lived. Helen's values and insights, in short, have intrinsic worth, even if some of them are distorted and only partly true. She is a complicated and fascinating character.

In a recent interview recorded by Furbank in *Writers at Work* (28), Forster asserted that he brought off the home life of Leonard and Jacky Bast, though he knew nothing at firsthand about it.[8] I agree with critics who find Leonard convincing for what he does; with I. A. Richards who, in "A Passage to Forster," finds him "horribly alive" (920); with Frederick Hoffman who, in "*Howards End* and the Bogey of Progress," regards him as a "most remarkable portrait, a mixture of hero and caricature" (252); and with James Hall who, in "Forster's Family Reunions," regards him as one of Forster's "best achievements" (28). In any event, Forster admirably projects into the sequences including Leonard and Jacky the elements of tenderness, squalor, humor, and vulgarity.

When Leonard is presented in action, he is a vital and interesting character. Forster, however, deflates him unnecessarily by belittling comment. It is difficult to understand why Forster thinks it is reprehensible for a poor man to have cultural ambitions. Actually, Leonard has, as Cyrus Hoy maintains in "Forster's Metaphysical Novel," the qualities in latent form that make Margaret heroic—"honor, courage, strength" (130). There is implied a link between the two when they both cut fingers on framed portraits. Leonard is also linked to Helen by virtue of the Cupid figurines on his lodging mantlepiece; we recall Helen's musing on the Cupids in the fretted ceiling of the concert hall and deciding she could never marry a man like them. In a moment of vehemence, it can be inferred, she later gives herself to a man she could never bring herself to marry.

Actually, Forster's treatment of Leonard is at once deft and heavy-handed. At the close of the novel, Leonard is beaten by Charles with the flat of Ernst Schlegel's sword in a parody of the knighthood ceremony. This effective use of a heroic ritual emphasizes the nonheroic qualities of Charles and Leonard. Leonard's death, as it derives from the toppled Schlegel bookcase, is, however, much too contrived, in making him a victim of the culture he sought. Elsewhere in the novel, Leonard is more convincingly a victim of pressures beyond his power to control. At Oniton, for example, his shabbiness contrasts with the opulence of Evie's wedding; this scene suggests that the impersonal laws by which the Wilcoxes smugly prosper have operated at the expense of Leonard and his class.

As for Henry Wilcox, critics generally agree that he is one of Forster's best creations. There is little question of Henry's reality, and Forster analyzes acutely his motives and personality. Forster conveys well his sexual charm, his forthright energy, and his commanding presence, depicting him as a surviving feudal lord of sorts who demands admiration from his family and the women he "protects." Forster establishes his insensitivity, his distrust of emotion, his evasiveness and lack of candor, his deficiency in generosity and in imagination, his complacency, and his inability to take criticism. On the whole, a negative impression emerges and a convincing one. This negative valuation, however, goes counter to the achievements, physical and moral, which Forster imputes to the Wilcoxes as empire-builders and developers of wealth.

A major flaw is Forster's failure to illustrate the Wilcox virtues n sequences as symbolically arresting as those in which he exemplifies the Wilcox defects. His customary subtlety fails him, and he relies too easily upon lyrical descriptions of the England which the Wilcoxes have helped build to suggest their positive traits. One ends by recognizing the truth of the Wilcox portraits in the novel but also by feeling that this truth applies to a certain kind of businessman and empire-builder, not to men in this class as a whole.

Critics such as F. R. Leavis, H. J. Oliver, and J. K. Johnstone have therefore considered Margaret's marriage to Henry as improbable or reprehensible. Yet Henry's animal magnetism and his energies are never in question; and they provide a firm basis for Margaret's yielding to him. It is natural enough that opposites like Henry and Margaret should be attracted and have a union which is happy on the surface and that it be fundamentally disturbed when their opposed values clash. The critics who have emphasized the "unreality" of the marriage have not fully appreciated, perhaps, the strains inherent in relationships involving temperamental opposites.[9] The presentation of Henry's and Margaret's life together is vulnerable, however, to the extent that Forster allows his own antipathy to Henry to outrun his intellectual valuation of Henry's type—in contrast with previous judgments, to describe him, for example, through Margaret after the fiasco over Helen, as "rotten at the core."

The characters in *Howards End* are arresting, the ideas conveyed are stimulating, and the organization is subtle. Yet the most lasting impression derives from Forster's brilliant style, which in its happiest reaches attains an incandescent realization of the actual, or an intensity associated with visionary experience. Light, color, and sound form the fabric of a prose which suggests more than it states and which opens out to the transcendent through the illuminated perceptions of the present moment.

The poetry is authentic in such sequences and scenes as Margaret's listening to the motions of the tidal waters on the Thames embankment, the colorful Maytime garden at Howards End on Margaret's first visit, the mist-enshrouded landscape and the ceaseless murmuring of the river at Oniton Grange, Margaret's walk at Hilton on her second visit to Howards End through the chestnut grove to the old church, and the enchanted moonlight night at the house when the sisters are united. Such scenes do suggest that Margaret's "belief in the eternity of beauty" is no idle or sentimental formulation. Such scenes convey to us, if fleetingly, "glimpses of the diviner wheels" (330), suggestions of the "ultimate harmony" we may be moving toward, and some notion that certain sense experiences are at times "apparelled in celestial light, / The glory and the freshness of a dream."

CHAPTER 5

"A Universe . . . not . . . Comprehensible to Our Minds": A Passage to India

I   A Novelist "of Delicacy and Resource": Forster as Comic Ironist

THE general judgment can stand that A *Passage to India* is Forster's best novel.[1] More than in his other works, Forster reveals a disciplined intelligence, an intellectual consistency, an expertise of craftsmanship, a firm design, a full articulation of a complex vision, a subtlety of thought, and a memorable evocation of empire and the Indian subcontinent. While we can recognize its preeminence, we need not, therefore, reject the earlier fiction; and we may even regret in A *Passage to India* a loss of freshness, creative zest, and fullness of character portrayal. One chief strain in the earlier work, that of ironical comedy, is present in A *Passage to India;* but the comedy deepens to achieve a metaphysical significance mostly latent in Forster's preceding books.

Ostensibly, he explores the relationships between the English administrators of empire and the Indian people they control. He presents the Anglo-Indian officials—Turton, Burton, McBryde, Major Callendar, and their womenfolk—satirically, but other English people like Mrs. Moore and Fielding he treats with sympathy. The reverent Mrs. Moore impresses Doctor Aziz, the mercurial Moslem, almost in spite of himself when he encounters her at night in the mosque at Chandrapore. Mrs. Moore is in India as companion to Adela Quested, who is engaged to Ronny Heaslop, one of the ruling Anglo-Indians and Mrs. Moore's son. Aziz invites the two ladies, the Hindu educator Godbole, and Fielding, the British principal of the local Indian college, to a picnic at the Marabar Caves, several miles distant from Chandrapore. In the caves, Mrs. Moore undergoes a total disillusionment; and Adela experiences either panic or hallucination and accuses Aziz of assault. The last half of the book traces the repercussions of this incident and of Adela's retraction of her charges against Aziz.

Ironic detachment, controlled satire, and an appreciation of comic incongruities inform Forster's presentation of social, imperial, and racial issues. "The bridge party" at the British Club, which Turton arranges for Miss Quested and Mrs. Moore, reveals Forster as a comic writer alive to the tragic meaning of racial misunderstanding. The failure of the party to "bridge" the races is ironic, and the rudeness of Mrs. Turton to her native guests has sinister as well as ludicrous overtones. Her advice to Adela Quested and Mrs. Moore—to remember that they are "superior to everyone in India except one or two of the Ranis, and they're on an equality"—comments implicitly on her arrogance and her limited sympathies; and Forster in his description of her use of Urdu ("to speak to her servants, so she knew none of the politer forms and of the verbs only the imperative mood") is the witty satirist who conveys implicitly the spiritual deficiencies of the English rulers of India.

Only after the English community has been roused by Aziz' imputed sexual insolence does Forster reveal fully his powers as ironic commentator upon a tense social situation. The irony is both verbal and dramatized. At this point, Adela's effect on the Anglo-Indians is described with asperity as bringing out "all that was fine in their character" (179); and Adela herself is subject to satiric scrutiny when Forster views the resumption of "her morning kneel to Christianity" as an indication of her desire to be reassured that "God who saves the King will surely support the police" (211).

The ironies inherent in the situations are manifold. The subaltern at the club praises the Indian with whom he has recently played at polo without knowing that the prisoner he condemns is this same man. Then, too, the questions arising from Adela's case loom so much greater to the English than do her misfortunes that inevitably her countrymen forget her as a person. Police Commissioner McBryde prosecutes Aziz by citing his theory that all people born south of thirty degrees latitude are promiscuous. But he has been having an illicit affair with Miss Derek and is guilty of a transgression similar to the one for which he is prosecuting an innocent man. And Aziz, although at Fielding's instigation he renounces his claims upon Adela, is never given credit for this act and is, on the contrary, assumed henceforth to be guilty of the offense for which he has been acquitted. The farcical intrudes

when the English are ordered from the platform of the courtroom
to which they had removed when Adela needed air. The Anglo-
Indians experience outrage because they sense a loss to their pres-
tige in having to obey the timorous request of the native magis-
trate.

Pervasive irony results from McBryde's courtroom mention of
Mrs. Moore as another lady whom Aziz may have insulted at the
picnic. McBryde thereby damages his own case; for when her relationship to Aziz causes heated discussion, her name is invoked
by the crowd outside. Now that Adela is reminded of her clair-
voyant friend, she perceives that Aziz is innocent, as Mrs. Moore
had earlier declared him to be. Consternation for the Anglo-
Indians and jubilation for the natives follow on Adela's retraction.
Always, then, in style and substance, distinctive modulations occur which reveal the presence of the dispassionate yet sympathetic analyst of human inconsistencies and of the corruptions to
which the exercise of power leads. The Anglo-Indians are exposed
the more mercilessly for the reason that they are not attacked directly. Forster perhaps best conveys, through his description elsewhere of Mrs. Gaskell's work, the nature of his own complex
comic art and of his own distinction as a novelist: "There are
plenty of the masterly muddles and the semi-quarrels and the
shifting of positions which are essential to comedy and which
can only be contrived by novelists of delicacy and resource." [2]

II *The "Double Vision" and the Tentative Hindu Synthesis*

A Passage to India is important for its social and political implications and for its revelations of Forster's luminous intelligence.
Nevertheless, the book's appeal is primarily esthetic, symbolic,
and philosophical. Forster's creative imagination, as it illuminates
the elemental aspects of humanity, results in this novel's richness.
Forster saw his book as metaphysical rather than social in impact
since he "tried to indicate the human predicament in a universe
which is not, so far, comprehensible to our minds." [3] The book exists chiefly as a vibrant esthetic entity which comments implicitly
upon issues that are universal in their significance. In its approach
to the transcendent, *A Passage to India* reaches romance and
prophecy; but it does so without sacrifice of social verisimilitude.

The "double vision," which bridges the extremities of existence,
expresses Forster's main preoccupation in *A Passage to India*. He

conjoins opposites as he did earlier; but in A *Passage to India* the mediation is an ongoing process for which only tentative resolutions exist. The exertions of the individual's will are important; so is the quality of the individual's mind and sensibility. For the superficial individual, guided only by his intellect, the possibility of attaining unity will not occur, or it will seem unimportant. Only an individual with developed powers of intuition can grasp the polarities of experience and see them in their true relationships.

When such polarities are continually present to the consciousness, truth is seen to be paradoxical. So throughout the book the complex qualities of ultimate reality and of God are stressed; so is a complex attitude toward nature and the primitive. So, too, is the ambivalent aspect of the caves and the Gokul Ashtami festival; so, too, is the elusive personality of Narayan Godbole, the individual who most often expresses a convoluted view of reality or dramatizes it in his conduct. So, too, is Mrs. Moore as a woman who is repelled by life in India but who grasps its essence.

Godbole's Hinduism takes us beyond good and evil to a cosmic force more often passive than positive and always unpredictable. At Fielding's party, Professor Godbole explains that his song is a lament for the God who does not come; and, in reply to Mrs. Moore, he explains further that no song exists which celebrates His certain coming. Following the disaster at the Marabar Caves, Godbole is still more explicit to Fielding. "Absence implies presence," Godbole says, though the two are not the same. Yet absence is not "non-existence," so we can say, "Come, come, come, come," in the hope that at some time the Divine may descend. Just as absence and presence are related, so are good and evil as aspects of the Divine. Both together, not either one separately, express the total universe. To desire the one without acknowledging the power of the other is to falsify. In the caves, Mrs. Moore is, unwittingly, the victim of simplified notions. She is immobilized because she finds God in his absent aspect when she had been too eager for God in his present aspect. Godbole, on the other hand, knows God's presence in "Temple" because he is less anxious to find Him and because he perceives that God will inevitably soon again be absent from him. Godbole is, in short, mystically more sophisticated than his English counterpart, Mrs. Moore.

Evil is not to be desired but to be endured, since its presence presupposes also the existence of good which will in its turn dominate. Good and evil are also universal human characteristics. When an evil act is performed, everyone has done it, Godbole asserts. So, if Adela were affronted in the cave, everyone who knew her shares complicity, whether or not he was present in the cave. Even Adela is in part guilty, as she sometimes senses when she heeds her deepest instincts instead of her intellect.

Godbole is a reconciling agent, wise but passive, intense yet indifferent. His mien suggests an imperturbable confidence, the result both of effort and of effortless vision: ". . . his whole appearance suggested harmony—as if he had reconciled the products of East and West, mental as well as physical, and could never be discomposed" (72). He also has a preternatural insight which none of the other characters possess, except in part for Mrs. Moore. Like his fellow Hindus, Godbole is preoccupied with the Unseen, and this description by Forster of the Hindu temperament accurately depicts Godbole:

The Hindu is concerned not with conduct, but with vision. To realise what God is seems more important than to do what God wants. He has a constant sense of the unseen—of the powers around if he is a peasant, of the power behind if he is a philosopher, and he feels that this tangible world, with its chatter of right and wrong, subserves the intangible.[4]

One who beholds the beatific vision can, like Godbole, die to the world and refuse to act in conformity to social pressures; one who beholds the horrific vision can, like Mrs. Moore, die to the world, refuse to help her friends, and long for her own death.

Mrs. Moore, who misunderstands her vision in the Marabar, dies before she can see it in true perspective. Alone, she is unable to reach the reality symbolized by the Hindu temple where all life forms emerge: "life human and superhuman and subhuman and animal, life tragic and cheerful, cruel and kind, seemly and obscene."[5] At the temple's apex is the sun which expresses the unity underlying these forms and the unity to which they aspire. It is the underside of this unity which Mrs. Moore encounters in the caves; and it is only in death that she attains the knowledge of all sides of it.

Her stature increases when she, at death, is translated into an Indian deity with powers similar to, and possibly exceeding, Godbole's own. In mythic terms she becomes a goddess who saves

Aziz at the trial, who brings the truth to Adela, who brings healing rains and fertility to the parched land by the sacrifice of her
life, and who reconciles East and West through her surviving influence in the minds of Aziz and Godbole and in the personalities
of her children, Ralph and Stella. This redemptive aspect of Mrs.
Moore is not inconsistent with her mystical sensitivity in the first
pages of the book; but she must endure a spiritual crucifixion before she can exert transcendent power. She is buried in the ocean
before she becomes a Hindu goddess, just as the image of Shri
Krishna must be thrown into the Mau tank before he can exert his
reanimating strength. As Ellin Horowitz suggests in her article
(81), Mrs. Moore atones for the rape of India by her countrymen
through saving the life of an Indian accused of assaulting an English woman.

By virtue of his Hinduism Godbole divines the complex relationships between himself and an unseen power beyond the here
and now. Fact to Hinduism is less important than the intangible,
as Forster had seen in 1914: "Greece, who has immortalised the
falling dust of facts, so that it hangs in enchantment for ever, can
bring no life to a land that is waiting for the dust to clear away, so
that the soul may contemplate the soul." [6] Although Godbole does
not figure greatly in the action, he is the chief source of truth.[7]

If Godbole provides Forster with some of his standards, Forster
does not accept Hinduism uncritically. The philosophical drift of
Hinduism interests Forster more than its ceremonies; like Mrs.
Moore's children, Ralph and Stella, he is drawn to Hinduism but
unconcerned about its forms. In 1919 Forster summarized his ambiguous views about the Hindu temple, substantially as he dramatizes them in the novel. The temple, and by implication Hinduism, violates our sense of the fitting, the beautiful, the human, and
the humane; but it is a building which, if we cannot love, we
cannot forget:

When we tire of being pleased and of being improved, and of the
other gymnastics of the West, and care, or think we care, for Truth
alone; then the Indian Temple exerts its power, and beckons down
absurd or detestable vistas to an exit unknown to the Parthenon.[8]

On balance, Hinduism means more to Forster than either Islam
or Christianity. In *The Hill of Devi* (127) he commends Islam for

its order and criticizes Hinduism for its disorder. But in the 1960's he could disparage Islam for its "orderliness." [9] In the novel he asserts that "the shallow arcades" of the mosque do not take us very deep into religious mysteries nor does Islam's primary belief, "There is no God but God"; and he refers scornfully to the "poor, talkative Christianity" that had been Mrs. Moore's solace before she entered the Marabar Caves. The alien energy and profusion present in the Gokul Ashtami ceremonies correspond to Forster's view of them expressed elsewhere as comprising "the strangest and strongest Indian experience ever granted me." [10]

Forster reveals a still more positive affinity with Hinduism when he describes himself on "nearer nodding terms with Krishna than with any other god," and when he perceives the power of Hinduism over skeptical temperaments such as his own: "it has caught sceptics at all times, and wrings cries of acquiescence and whispers of hope." [11] In Hinduism, Forster finds an encompassing reality that unifies the world and binds together animate and inanimate life, an impersonal spiritual force with which one can identify mystically, and a belief in love as a binding spiritual and moral value—a "love in which there neither was nor desired to be sensuality, though it was excited at the crisis and reached ecstasy." [12]

III   *The Marabar Caves: "Illusion . . . Set Against the Background of Eternity"*

The Marabar Caves embody the neutral substratum of the universe and lack positive attributes.[13] Just as Hinduism takes us philosophically to a plane beyond good or evil, so the caves exist physically—insofar as natural objects can—in a void, having been created before space and time began. They contain, therefore, a primordial reality, basic to all later differentiations of being, animate or inanimate, in space or time. Godbole intuitively knows this truth about the caves, but at Fielding's tea party he senses that his Moslem and Occidental audience would not understand it if he were now to describe it. Godbole realizes that in the caves one may have perceptions which reach "straight back into the universal, to a blackness and sadness so transcending our own that they are undistinguishable from glory" (*Aspects of the Novel*, 143). In these words, whereby Forster expresses the concern of Melville and other prophetic writers, he characterizes the intui-

tions of Godbole, the formidable negations experienced by Mrs.
Moore in the Marabar, and the affirmations she fails to find there.

If the inmost caves were to be excavated, nothing would be
added to the sum of good and evil, Forster explains; yet good and
evil, and all other polarities, are in the caves.[14] The reality the
caves enclose can be extended in a negative or a positive direction
as circumstances or the powers of the individual permit. They
were created before pestilence or treasure, Forster says; but pestilence and treasure, and all such contrarieties, develop from them.

The caves and hills are genuinely extraordinary and their meaning is elusive. Close at hand they present "a nasty little cosmos"; at
a distance, they seem finite and romantic and breathe a promise of
spiritual renewal. Everything in the world possesses equal value,
the caves assert through their confounding echo; and there is
nothing special, then, about man and his aspirations. If man is
equal to all other things, he has no special value in himself but is
as valuable as all other manifestations of existence, valuable as a
wasp, a snake, or a sun-burnt rock. He is not necessarily at the
apex of a great chain of being or a little less than the angels.
Godbole knows that the world was not made for man, but Mrs.
Moore's Christianity does not allow her to see that far.

Fearsome as the caves are in their aboriginal darkness, when a
light is struck the beauties of the reflected flames are like "exquisite nebulae." What had seemed completely dark is the source
of light; and the caves, with their rough exterior surface, possess
hidden beauty. The struggles of the flame within the granite walls
to reach the source of light without are symbolic of the efforts of
Godbole, Mrs. Moore, and some of the others to let their human
fires merge with a divine fire. And the radiance increases as image
and flame seemingly touch each other and "kiss" before they ex-
pire, just as the soul expires when in Hinduism it is merged with
the world soul to achieve its Nirvana.

The powers of nullity are too strong for the English women to
withstand at the Marabar. The caves overwhelm them, saddling
Mrs. Moore with disillusion and Adela with delusion. There the
eternal and the infinite lack beauty and sublimity, and become
ugly and timeless. The Unseen achieves expression not only in the
unsettling echo but in such a phenomenon as the cheeping of the
mangy squirrels outside Aziz' house before the picnic. During the
hot weather at least, the infinite has no link with exaltation, es-

thetic or spiritual. The two women feel isolated from other people and from each other; and the caves intensify and bring to focus their latent frustrations: Mrs. Moore's doubts about her usefulness as a human being; Adela's misgivings about sex and love.

The concept of eternity becomes equivalent in the caves to an "undying worm," and this worm or serpent is full of crawling maggots. Insofar as the serpent is emblematic of the life principle, it is contorted and twisted; life, as seen from the perspective of the caves, recoils on itself and has no purposeful motion. Even Shri Krishna, a life-god in Hinduism, had once appeared as a sinister serpent to churn the seas in order to form the nectar of immortality and, incidentally, to mix together into a chaos the forms of creation.[15] To Mrs. Moore, life, seen purposefully, retreats before the echo's expression of chaos, disorder, and negation. As yet, she has no power to see that chaos and disorder betoken life as well as death, and imply, by their very existence, the existence of their opposites. Men can endure only so much of the negation which Mrs. Moore finds in the echo before they retreat into the self. The echo muffles Mrs. Moore's spirit, just as a direct view of God might have blinded her.

The Unseen is sinister only when one is confronted starkly with it. If, as Fielding says, "the echo is always evil," that which the echo emanates from need not be. If one penetrates the echo, he may not be totally reassured; but he will, likely as not, find a reality that is more than negative. But reality remains hidden and can only be grasped evanescently, even by the adept.[16] Preparatory to her visit to the caves, Mrs. Moore sees the universe as a series of receding arches with an echo beyond the last arch, and then a silence. The silence is evidently Eternity, impassive but not hostile; the echo in its reverberation is more malign than the silence. The wise man accepts the universe as it is; and he sees that its apparent evils, if overpowering, need not be permanent. Arch and echo are expanding and retracting images which connect the individual, sometimes against his will, with an eternity more ominous than reassuring. Yet the existence of the Eternal, however veiled to human eyes, argues for a measure of stability and meaning in a chaotic universe.

Fielding and Adela do not understand the mysteries inherent in the hills or the terrors inherent in the caves; but they do have glimmers of perception. The Anglo-Indians, who have none at all, are unequal to India and think, for example, that its irrational energies can be controlled by numbering the Marabar Caves with paint to distinguish one from another. The antagonism between Ronny and his mother, particularly after Aziz' arrest, indicates his failure to comprehend the irrational forces which now sway her.

Ronny is not at home anywhere in India, in mosque, caves, or temple ("Mosque," "Caves," and "Temple" are, in fact, the titles of the three successive divisions of the novel). He is symbolic of the rootless Anglo-Indian officials who lack not only Mrs. Moore's mystical awareness but Fielding's graciousness and humanity, Adela's sincerity, and Aziz' dedication to the personal. Those who attend Fielding's tea party would not be misfits in the "Mosque," but they would not understand (except for Godbole) the full implications of "Caves" or "Temple." Mrs. Moore, as we have seen, is a sacrificed god. She is also a sacrifice to the canons of propriety when Ronny sends her out of India to die from heat exhaustion on her homeward voyage. He hastens her death rather than risk her candor at Aziz' trial.

As Louise Dauner and Wilfred Stone both stress, the caves comprise the sum total of all experience—the locus of community activity and of burial rites, the womb and tomb of all existence, an archetype of the great mother and of annihilation.[17] In the caves one can discern the upward swirl of aspiration and the downward pull of fact, the life in the unconscious and the failure of the mind to comprehend this life. The caves include, moreover, all the rhythms of existence, especially the most basic, that of life versus death. It is sometimes difficult to disentangle the life from the death principle. One implies the other, just as absence asserts presence and evil, good. The caves, which embody death as well as life, are of "very dead and quiet" granite; and Mrs. Moore received one part of India's message, the disabling echo, in "that scoured-out cavity of the granite." Rock is refractory, although as Forster implies elsewhere (247), stones, as well as plants and animals, feel perhaps the pain of the universe and are potentially sentient. In *Alexandria* (71), Forster had said that for the Neo-Platonist all things are parts of God, including the stones; and he had implied, therefore, that some mystics had achieved a completeness greater than Godbole's. In Hinduism "completeness" matters, not "reconstruction," which may be too human in implication.

But even Professor Godbole cannot assimilate stones to his vision of cosmic unity though he can merge with Mrs. Moore, whom he only dimly remembers, and the wasp. The stones signify the difficulty in his attaining completeness of vision rather than, as McConkey (144) asserts, an inability to attain it. Another fact emerges: the negations of the Marabar cannot be assimilated to a philosophy less inclusive than that symbolized by the caves and hills. Hinduism, alone of the religions presented, has the comprehensiveness to absorb such realities.

As commentators have suggested, the caves relate to Hinduism.[18] The presence of caves in Hindu myths and rituals, the correspondence between illusions (such as those experienced in the Marabar) and the Hindu veils of Maya, the similarity of the echo sound to that of the mystic syllable "Om," and the presence of flame and serpent imagery at the Marabar and in Hindu scriptures alike link the Marabar Caves to Hinduism. One need not assert that Mrs. Moore has a Hindu vision there; rather she undergoes, as Forster says, "the vision . . . with its back turned." [19] The revelation to her is less a repudiation of Hinduism, however, than an apprehension of the negative aspect of its primal reality.

If the caves embody a life principle however contorted or disguised or remote from us, they also suggest the death principle. After too great an exposure to the forces let loose at the Marabar, the characters return to Chandrapore in a train that seems dead though it moves; and all the people in it are like corpses. The hills are seen as gods, and the earth is a ghost in comparison. So, as dwellers on the plain, we find that our mundane lives and values become illusory before the cosmic truth concentered in the hills; in their vicinity, "everything seemed cut off at its root, and therefore infected with illusion" (140).

Forster also agrees with a statement which he quotes in a review and which stresses the insignificance of our lives when compared to the transcendent: ". . . for in Indian art, as in Indian philosophy, all life, even the life of the gods, is an illusion or play set against the background of eternity." [20] Such a juxtaposition of meaning and nothingness is too difficult for Mrs. Moore and the non-Hindus in the novel to grasp entire. The dispelling of illusion and the confrontation of a first reality should, for the initiated, eventuate in knowledge and insight rather than in the disillusion suffered by Mrs. Moore. All of Mrs. Moore's spiritual constructs—

love, beauty, piety—now lack abiding force for her at the Marabar. They are man-made, abstract formulations, irrelevant to the
amoral, primordial essence of things, revealed both in the caves
and in Hinduism. The caves contain a reality that dispels Maya or
illusion, and they do so violently for the casual intruder, just as the
dwellers in the Platonic caves lose their illusions reluctantly when
confronted with the light. If cessation of life seems fearsome in
"Caves," death in "Temple" is a kinder force than it is in Europe,
"its pathos was less poignant, its irony less cruel . . . There was
death in the air, but not sadness; a compromise had been made
between destiny and desire, and even the heart of man acqui-
esced" (304, 307).

The hills—and by implication the caves which they cover—
overwhelm by excess; they lack the "proportion" seen even in the
most rugged hills elsewhere and deflect the aspiration for a comprehensible certitude. The caves and the negations undergone
there by the Western visitors are crucial. But the caves open out
to the Shri Krishna birth festivities and provide for their exuberance the most solid possible base. Just so the cave, with its sugges-
tion of mystery and the elemental, is at the heart of the temple.
But the cave is also subsumed by the entire temple which flaunts a
multi-faceted, inclusive rendition of outward forms. The anteced-
ent matrix of being, contained in the caves, is assimilated into
the total structure of creation. It is never lost, however, and we
must be prepared to acknowledge its violent, primitive effects. If
Hinduism has inclusiveness, it is not orderly: "Ragged edges of
religion . . . unsatisfactory and undramatic tangles . . . God si
love" (316).

This amorphousness permits Hinduism to absorb disillusionment and apathy, as well as creativity and joy—both the experiences that transfigure life and the knowledge that these experiences are also illusions that perish. If the ceremonies possess
"fatuity," they also possess "philosophy" (*The Hill of Devi*, 107).
In its widest reaches Hinduism would annihilate sorrow for all:
"not only for Indians, but for foreigners, birds, caves, railways,
and the stars; all became joy, all laughter; there had never been
disease nor doubt, misunderstanding, cruelty, fear" (288). Truly,
as Forster said in 1914, in the Hindu view of things "the divine is
so confounded with the earthly that anyone or anything is part of
God." [21] If caves induce in the unprepared individual a dynamic

nihilism, the temple festivities induce in the prepared individual a sense of cosmic unity and of dynamic life.

IV   A *"Bewildering . . . Echoing, Contradictory World"*

The structure of the novel illustrates its paradoxical content. Many readings, however, stress a "triadic" structure of thesis, acting upon antithesis, to produce a synthesis; and this kind of progression is not absent from the book.[22] The rational, sentimentalized views of God, such as the Moslem Aziz and the Christian Mrs. Moore express in "Mosque," crumble when an indifferent cosmos subdues Mrs. Moore and Adela Quested in "Caves." In turn, the spiritual lethargy induced by the Marabar and the evil forces of division let loose there yield partly in "Temple" to the mystical strengths of Hinduism, its emphasis upon love, and the breadth of its philosophy. Each section of the novel is, moreover, associated with one of the three principal seasons of the Indian year.[23] Still, the novel charts primarily the dualities of life as they exist in uneasy conjunction with one another rather than the transmutation of them into something else. All contrasting objects and mental states merge into the Unity underlying the universe, but they do not usually become something else midway in the process.

The motion of the novel is cyclic rather than linear; dialectical opposites are not resolved and continue indefinitely to exert their strength. Forster is at once preoccupied with a timeless unity and with the concrete manifestations of that unity in time. So at the end Aziz distrusts, then accepts, a cyclic explanation of his life; and he realizes that little enough has been resolved through his sufferings. His encounter with Ralph Moore induces a fear that the "Mosque"-"Caves" cycle may start again. He is far from reassured at the prospect but perceives that the inevitable cannot be avoided.

The dispelling of drought and suffering by the monsoon rains organizes the novel in terms of a cyclic fertility ritual, as Ellin Horowitz and Edgar A. Austin have suggested in their articles; and Mrs. Moore is, as we have seen, the god whose life must be sacrificed in order that the healing rains may descend. In this cyclic pattern, the progress is from affirmation to negation to qualified affirmation. Nothing is canceled. The same forces of division and unity still exist, but in "Temple" they are seen in a double aspect as temporal and eternal.

In "Temple," the affirmation is tentative and hard-earned. Mrs. Moore's assertion, "God is Love," in "Mosque" had been too complacent. The Hindu version of this same principle, "God si Love," is more flexible; the fact that the Hindu recognizes mundane chaos is implied in the misspelling of the verb. For him, love is more abstract, more transcendental, more removed from the individual's desires and ideals than for the Christian or the Moslem. Though infinite love is the basis for the Hindu religion, the Hindu regards "love" apart from the order and the precise formulations of the Western or Islamic mind.

Love for the Hindu is an experience at once more immediate and more remote, less fastidious and more far-reaching, than for other men. For Godbole indeed and for Mrs. Moore in her mystical moments, love extends to the wasps and, by implication, to all forms of animate life; and Godbole would include the inanimate, the stones of India, if he could manage to do so. The progression of the book is from light to darkness to modified light; the fact that illumination has come implies also that it may come again: "Hope existed despite fulfillment, as it will be in heaven" (303).

The nature of God himself, as the Hindu envisages it, is complex. In "Temple," Godbole is standing in the presence of God but removed from Him, at the other end of a carpet which distances Him from His worshipper. God, in short, exists; but He is difficult to know. All statements about Him are alike true and untrue: "He is, was not, is not, was" (283). God has not yet been born when the ceremonies begin; He will be born at midnight, but He was also born centuries ago; He can never be born perhaps, because, as the Lord of the Universe, He has always existed and transcends all human endeavors to encompass Him in creed or in ritual. At the height of the ceremonies, He is thrown into the water; but He can't be thrown away. Such are the ambiguous rituals which the Hindu observes, such the certainties and uncertainties inherent in all spiritual proceedings. The God to be thrown away and all other such images and symbols are, Forster says, "emblems of passage": "a passage not easy, not now, not here, not to be apprehended except when it is unattainable" (314).[24] In any event, God transcends the categories that we can formulate for Him. The participants in the Krishna ceremony worship a god without attributes because it would be presumptuous for human beings to affix attributes to him. Yet the truth exists that a god without attributes may be one who possesses all attributes.

Nature, another manifestation of the Unseen, is scarcely amenable to the human understanding. The Ganges seems glamourous in the moonlight to Mrs. Moore when she first visits India, but she is shocked to learn that crocodiles inhabit it. Now the river seems both terrible and wonderful. The night, though beautiful, is full of unrest; it is never tranquil, nor is it ever completely dark. The "jolly" jungle scenery at Mau conceals a deadly cobra, as Aziz and Fielding go on their final ride; the scenery, though it "smiles," places, as it were, a "gravestone on any human hope" (321). If nature is apparently indestructible, she is yet undergoing slow change and erosion; and gradually the plain will engulf the hills which are of "incredible antiquity" and "flesh of the sun's flesh." George H. Thomson's judgment in *The Fiction of E. M. Forster* is, I think, exactly right: "The awareness of one universe and the experience of oneness with that universe have become ideals more difficult to attain than they were in the past . . ." (205).

Nature is not only an imponderable force but a vital animating one as well—as the personification of the hills and Forster's use of the pathetic fallacy in describing them indicate. The hills both "lie flat" and "heave"; they "creep forward" to the city and "leap" to beauty at sunset; they thrust fists and fingers up to the sky; inside, the walls of the caves are skin to the fists and fingers; and the foothills are "knees" to the other hills. The surrounding caves and boulders proclaim that they are alive; and, when the intruders to the "queer valley" leave, "stabs" of hot air pursue them. If Grasmere is more manageable and more romantic than India, it is also less real and alive. Mrs. Moore, when she first comes to India and sees the moon in all its splendor, thinks how dead and alien it had seemed to her in England.

The punkah-wallah at the trial is a symbol of India's natural vitality. Under his impassive influence, Adela becomes aware of more than her own sufferings and is receptive to the double vision which awakens in her when Mrs. Moore's name is pronounced. The punkah-wallah, as an embodiment of the Life-Force, contrasts with "the serpent of eternity" known in the caves; Adela understands neither one fully, though each one disturbs her radically. The punkah-wallah, too, as Thomson (211) alleges, is the undifferentiated vital base of a spiritual pyramid at whose apex resides the articulate, sophisticated Godbole. The resplendent native who wades into the Mau tank during the tempest to consign the palanquin bearing Shri Krishna's image to the waves is, like the punkah-wallah, an emblem of primitive strength.

The truth is that India is both a muddle and a mystery, but a mystery that can only be reached through muddle. So the temple ceremonies are "a triumph of muddle," though they suggest certain transcendent truths. To those who experience her superficially, India seems vast and amorphous, a country where life abounds but where discernible purpose is absent: "There seemed no reserve of tranquillity to draw upon in India . . . or else tranquillity swallowed up everything" (78). To those who can penetrate the outward confusion, she proves to be a mystery and purveys certain truths. India's very size and multiple cultures prevent anyone from understanding her easily, let alone completely. The Indian countryside is too vast to admit of excellence; only from the remotest perspective, from the moon for instance, would India acquire at last a firm outline.

At the same time, categories in India are rigid and defeat the attempts made to bridge them: so the bridge party is a failure, and the picnic at the Marabar a fiasco when Aziz "challenged the spirit of the Indian earth, which tries to keep men in compartments" (127). The country is divided between Moslems and Hindus who do not understand one another; and even Hinduism fragments into a hundred dissenting sects. The numerous inflexible distinctions, found in Indian life, reinforce the impression of disunity and multiplicity produced by the landscape, the confused social patterns, and the many civilizations of the subcontinent.

Aziz' desire to encompass "the vague and bulky figure of a mother-land" (268) in his conversation and in his poems is mostly false, therefore, since his idea of the diversities and of the unity to be found in India is inadequate. For the Moslem, India can be perplexing; so Aziz' dead wife looks out from her portrait on a "bewildering . . . echoing, contradictory world," and Aziz in Mau dismisses the Hindu festival as remote from any sanctities of his own. The Indian culture and the Indian mind also baffle the rationalistic Westerner, leaving him "with the sense of a mind infinitely remote from ours—a mind patriotic and sensitive—and it may be powerful, but with little idea of logic or facts; we retire baffled, and, indeed, exasperated." [25] At no point, moreover, are the Westerners so confused, disturbed, and fascinated as by Godbole's impromptu song at Fielding's tea party. There is something equivocal and difficult about life in India which the sands of the Suez Canal and the Mediterranean countries wipe out as soon as one leaves the waters of the Orient. The Mediterranean civilization has escaped "muddle" and attained a true harmony, "with flesh and blood subsisting." From such a "norm" we depart as soon as we leave the Mediterranean, particularly if we leave it to the South where the "monstrous" and "extraordinary" are most likely to confront us, in India and the Orient in general. Western humanism is unable to explain India; it is too selective and too easily abashed by the stubborn facts. In India new categories are difficult to impose, intellectual discriminations are often impossible to make, the unaided powers of the mind are insufficient to comprehend a land so diverse. In India, as Forster says in *The Hill of Devi*, "everything that happens is said to be one thing and proves to be another" (64). In the East, the harmonies of Western art and religion are replaced by the dissonances of Hindu music, the teeming "world-mountain" of the Indian temple, and the sounds and confusions of the Gokul Ashtami rituals. The forms of Occidental art are attractive for the Western European; but, satisfying as they are for him, they yet represent only a partial view of reality.

The Gokul Ashtami festival represents a "frustration of reason and form" and a "benign confusion"; the participants reveal a "sacred bewilderment." No one knows precisely what happens, "whether a silver doll or a mud village, or a silk napkin, or an intangible spirit, or a pious resolution, had been born" (290). In "Temple," Forster makes esthetic use of chaos similar to Emily Brontë's use of it in *Wuthering Heights* (*Aspects of the Novel*, 145). Since, in Forster's view, Miss Brontë implied more than what she said, she had recourse to "muddle, chaos, tempest" to enable her characters to achieve through it the greatest degree of expressiveness for their superhuman experiences. So only in confusion can the Hindu religious rituals and the collision of the boats in the Mau tank during the tempest attain their ineffable implications. For the Eastern sensibility, vitality is surely more important than beauty. The Eastern mentality senses that the disorder of the universe presupposes an ultimate order: the conventional Western moralist or religionist would impose his own order upon the universe instead of responding to the strong chaotic currents within it which go beyond mere negation or mere affirmation.[26]

V *Imagery: "Irradiating Nature from Within"*

The image patterns in *A Passage to India* unify the novel. More subtly and insistently than in the early fiction, the method is symphonic. The three masses of the novel accumulate force and meaning through a polyphonic mounting of themes and images which reverberate in the mind and achieve symbolic expansion for the novel as it develops. The resolution is one that opens out rather than contracts. In discussing Lawrence as a prophetic writer in *Aspects of the Novel*, Forster reveals his own affinities with him. Judging his greatness to be esthetic rather than intellectual, Forster finds that Lawrence is "irradiating nature from within, so that every colour has a glow and every form a distinctness which could not otherwise be obtained" (144).

The irradiations are achieved in great part through the use of an imagery as evocative as that found in formal poetry. In Forster's view, sound or song is a principal component of prophetic fiction. As if to illustrate that his own book might be prophetic, Forster's most compelling images are auditory, from the "terrible gong" struck in the Marabar to the exuberant noises at Mau to the sounds, at once ominous and vital, heard in "Mosque" and elsewhere. These sounds convey the intense activities of a teeming nation and hint at the eruptive forces lying just below the surfaces of Oriental life; and they herald the presence—or the absence—of the Eternal. As in Melville's books, Forster's own "prophetic song," expressed primarily through Godbole, "flows athwart the action and the surface morality like an undercurrent" (*Aspects of the Novel*, 138).

An imagery based upon the "four elements," earth (rock), air, fire (heat, sun), and water predominates and strengthens the impression that *A Passage to India* elaborates elemental themes—is, in a word, "prophetic." The ambiguity informing ideal value extends as well to image patterns. The fires of the stars are friendly, the hills at Mau have many temples "like little white flames," the reflected flames in the polished granite walls of the caves are the sole source of beauty there, and the "exquisite nebulae" of these flames connect with the torches that "star" the farther shore of the lake when the Krishna images are consigned to the water. Stars connect also with Mrs. Moore and her beneficent influence: we remember, for example, her early mystical raptures when she gazes at the heavens, the presence of the stars on the acquittal night when Fielding and Aziz discuss her reported death, and the name of her daughter, Stella. Genuine warmth, moreover, characterizes the Shri Krishna ceremonies over which a friendly sun prevails.

But the fire images have negative meaning as well. The Anglo-Indians at the time of Aziz' arrest are "fired" by their intolerance; Turton is "fused by some white and generous heat"; the image of the ethereal and defenseless Mrs. Blakiston remains in the mind of the ladies "like a sacred flame"; "a not unpleasant glow" pervades the Anglo-Indians as they make ready to defend the purity of their homes-from outward menace. The picnic, arrest, and trial take place in April, "herald of horrors," when the sun returns to tropic lands "with power but without beauty" and when "irritability and lust" prevail. Mrs. Moore resents the "barrier of fire" that will keep her "bottled up" in the hot weather; she is a victim of heat prostration after she traverses India in May. At the caves, "films of heat" descend capriciously from the Kawa Dal and "a patch of field would jump up as if it was being fried" (141); and the visitors enter the caves with "the sun crashing on their backs" (146).

A similar complexity marks the references to the air, the earth, and the water. The air at night, especially in the first and third parts of the novel, is sweet, cool, and friendly; and it contrasts with the air at the caves that feels "like a warm bath into which hotter water is trickling constantly" (150). But the air from the punkah-wallah's fan at the trial sweeps Adela on to a proclamation of the truth and gives her courage; at the end of the book, the air is "thick with religion and rain," (298) ostensibly in harmony with human aspirations and the renewal of the earth's fertility; and the freshening gale brings the boats on the Mau tank together and leads to the reconciliation of the Indians and the English.

The sky has also beauty and serenity which shade off at times into hostility. At the storming of the hospital after the trial when "the spirit of evil again strode ahead," (235) the earth and sky are "insanely ugly"; at the caves, the sky dominates and seems "unhealthily near." But, at the end, the beautiful sunset sky is reflected in the Mau water tank; and pleasing white clouds and purple hills in the distance give a tranquil setting for Fielding's last ride with Aziz. The overspreading sky is a symbol of infinitude in space as the hills are a symbol of infinitude in time; both furnish vistas that terrify the mind but please the imagination—arch following upon arch, through the immense vault where hang the stars to the endless space beyond. The new geology and the new astronomy of the nineteenth century find their unerring correlatives, then, in the Marabar Hills and in the reaches of the sky above them. The sky is all powerful and "settles everything" and it can express unity and division both. Depending on the changes that take place there, the earth below becomes fruitful or barren, luxuriant or stony.

Similarly, the earth both nourishes and destroys. It is malignant at the Marabar Caves, which are set in a desert wasteland where earth vaunts its strength in the granite rock of the hills. But the same earth nourishes the lush jungle at Mau with its "jolly" vegetation and park-like beauty. Even the parched land about Bombay does not seem so lifeless to Mrs. Moore as had the Indian plain, because man and his "indestructible life" are not absent from it; now she can view the country for what it is, not for the way it refracts her inner agonies to her. Earth, finally, is the nourishing mother who bestows "myriads of kisses" as she draws the water of the monsoon into her inmost being.

The water images suggest the ceaseless flux of life in India, and can betoken its potential horror or its possible gift of peace. At the caves the sultry atmosphere that feels like hot water has been mentioned; also, when one enters a cave, he is sucked into it like water going down a drain. Adela remembers that "the pale masses of the rock [at the Marabar] flowed round her" (228) as an enveloping flood and that the echo in the caves "had spouted after her when she escaped, and was going on still like a river that gradually floods the plain" (194). The floods may also act as a divisive factor.

But, generally, the rains relieve the drought and are a friendly if an elemental force. The festival flows on as a collective activity, potentially uniting all men; on the waters of the tank, the boats collide, and their occupants are thrown together to be reconciled as the tray bearing Krishna's image strikes the boats. The tray next comes near Godbole, who, a kind of magician, has presided over the ceremonies and the accident. To indicate his unity with both the human and divine, with the mundane and the transcendent, he smears upon his forehead some of the remaining mud from which the sacred images on the tray had been fashioned. The kissing sounds of the bats at the tanks also connote the healing effects exuding from the waters. Water also acts as a uniting symbol through the various tanks in the novel, one at each important locale: at the Mosque, at Fielding's garden, at the Marabar Caves, and at Mau. The tanks imply that in basic ways the races of mankind are one: physically, water satisfies a universal need; and, spiritually, when used in baptismal rites or other sacramental rituals, it also binds the races of man.

VI *Intelligence versus Intuition: Forster's Characters*

The chief characters in the novel, other than Godbole, are seen in terms of their reactions to the Marabar and the Gokul Ashtami festival; but they also exist powerfully as human beings. The caves and the temple ceremonies symbolize, respectively, the destructive and the creative forces underlying our life in society and in nature. They also represent the unconscious and its complexities; and, to the degree the individual comprehends the caves and temple, he achieves wholeness. Response to the truths of the unconscious is, however, often disappointing, for, as Wilfred Stone states, "Consciousness and unconsciousness pursue each other in the novel, but they do not meet—and therein lies the world tragedy" (310). And, when they do meet, they meet to part, except as the individual can look forward with the years to an increased sense of the true proportions of life or to religious transfiguration. Quite simply, we do not achieve often enough for our spiritual well-being the fusion of will and creative power, of sense impressions and vision, of abstraction and prophecy. Of the characters, only Mrs. Moore and Godbole strain toward the mythic and the archetypal and reach the deepest sources of unconscious knowledge. The others move within fixed outlines of their preconceptions, the nuances of which, however, are defined in relationship to the mythic and elemental aspects of the book.

Aziz, regarded by critics as Forster's most brilliant creation, is contradictory and complicated; and he is the only exhaustively developed character. He is sensitive rather than responsive, but sensitive in a self-centered way, sensitive almost to the point of paranoia. He inclines, therefore, to suspicion rather than to trust; and his relationships with Fielding deteriorate when he suspects the Englishman of love for Adela Quested (thus Aziz explains Fielding's plea that he give up suing Adela for damages). Aziz, motivated by "the secret understanding of the heart," is far more spontaneous in his relationships than is Fielding, but this spontaneity misleads because it is uncritical. Although his "adoration" of Mrs. Moore runs deep, he is capable of cruelty to her son Ralph because of his own abstract hatred for the English and his unjust disappointment in Fielding. Like the earlier Mrs. Moore, Aziz is something of a romantic and attains his vision of harmony too readily, as he drops off to sleep and dreams of his joys flourishing without hindrance in "an eternal garden."

In his adoration of Mrs. Moore and in his effusiveness toward Ralph her son, he senses depths of being he does not otherwise sound (extending his hand to Ralph, he is "focusing his heart on something more distant than the caves, something beautiful" [311]). Although he is mostly a figure whose strength is realistic, he does have the mythic dimensions suggested by Ellin Horowitz (80): he is regarded by the Anglo-Indians as a demon lover and as a "dark rapist" of a violated virgin or white goddess.

The Western intellect, like the Moslem, is inadequate for an understanding of the Marabar—of truths reached by intuition. Aziz and Fielding are rationalists, despite Aziz' emotional nature and Fielding's magnanimity. Both men need the mellowing which mystical experience alone can give; they remain distrustful of the intuitive, although they achieve their best moments through its means. After the arrest when Fielding goes against the Anglo-Indians to defend Aziz, he feels a momentary affinity with the supernal forces concentrated in the hills; and, as a result of his wife's interest in Hinduism, he feels their union is "blessed" at last. Aziz, of course, is at his most admirable when he recalls the profound Mrs. Moore and abandons the petty side of his nature.

Fielding senses the reality of India more accurately than Adela Quested, his compatriot; he sees it as a manifold entity and advises the credulous Adela to get to know Indians rather than India. As a humanist, he believes in reason; and for him the clarity of intellect is a primary value. He is, as Wilfred Stone suggests, a Bloomsbury intellectual let loose in India, "liberal, decent, and sensitive" (326). As such, he dislikes the muddle which he sees everywhere in India; and its insistent mystery usually makes him uncomfortable.

Fielding continually has misgivings about his rational values. After his repudiation of Ronny Heaslop at the club, he looks at the hills and perceives, despite the order he has imposed on his life, that something is missing from it and that he may never find out what. Hints of an idealistic view of the world, which he cannot fully probe, visit him; we exist, he thinks, only in terms of each other's minds, though this is not a logical premise. He wants to discover the "spiritual side" of Hinduism, although he pursues this inquiry too intellectually; and he wishes to comprehend, perhaps too directly, the mystical elements in his wife's personality.

As descendants of the visionary Mrs. Moore, Stella and Ralph share their mother's sensitivity to the ineffable. Fielding knows that Stella aspires to kinds of insight he does not fully understand. Under the influence of Hinduism Stella attains calm and transfers some of it to Fielding. Their union is now strengthened because the "link outside either participant," needed for a firm relationship, has been forged. Their union thus represents a true marriage of the rational and the intuitive. The symbolic marriage in *A Passage to India* is far more convincing than the marriages in *A Room with a View* and *Howards End* which have similar meaning. The as yet unborn child in *A Passage to India* is a more promising prophetic figure than Helen's 'boy in *Howards End*. In the future, perhaps, the polar qualities of our own existence can be united more readily in a single personality than they can be now.

Reconciliation is still possible in this life, despite the sundered relationship between Aziz and Fielding—the "tragic separation of people who part before they need, or who part because they have seen each other too closely." [27] The parting involves a salutary recognition, by Aziz and Fielding, of the truth. The courage needed to face the inevitable may well be the quality needed to unite people. The "not yet" of the last paragraph implies an opposite state: the future fruition and union. The temple door shuts as the men take their last ride, implying an end of the concord between them: yet the door will some time open again and the divisions of daily life be transcended. Stella Moore in these pages is, like her mother, a wise priestess. To Fielding, she pronounces that the

Marabar is wiped out, as a result of the boat collision; and Aziz emphasizes this truth by using the same words when he writes his letter to Adela. The reconciliation in the last pages is real but incomplete.

As a human being, Fielding is interesting and admirable; and one must agree with George H. Thomson (226) that "the limited achievement" of Fielding and Adela counts for more than their failures. Fielding, a humanist, believes in the power of "good will plus culture and intelligence." If excess clarity is his flaw, he uses his reason to disarm the herd instinct and to combat the psychology of the mob. He is both "hard-bitten" and "good tempered"; and, if he lacks religious sensibility and recoils from open emotional display, he has tact and social imagination. He is popular with his students, he stays with the Indians at the bridge party, and he removes most of the obstacles to free discourse between himself and the typical Indian, Aziz. His flexible intelligence and his respect for ideas render him unpopular with those exponents of a rigid intellect, the Anglo-Indians. Although Fielding may be cynical about such relationships as marriage, his cynicism is superficial. It does not deter him from marriage or from conscientiousness in his ties with others. He is truly, as he says, a "holy man minus the holiness," a kind man suspicious of the ecstatic; and he travels somewhat less "light" than he thinks he does.

Adela Quested is excessively intellectual and humorless, too abstract in temper to attain profundity. She believes conscientiously in the sanctity of human relationships and tries sincerely to establish rapport with others. But such efforts derive from the will instead of the heart, so that she is unable to give effective expression to her ideals. She has an absolute honesty but lacks the imagination to render her honesty notable. She thus perceives that she was wrong to substitute tenderness, respect, and personal liking for love in her relationships with Ronny.

The experience in the caves is crucial to Adela. On the surface of her mind she thinks that Aziz is guilty: "the echo flourished, raging up and down like a nerve in the faculty of her hearing, and the noise in the cave, so unimportant intellectually, was prolonged over the surface of her life" (194). But when she gets beyond reason, she sees her actions more truly than when she thinks about them; and, in Mrs. Moore's real or imagined presence, the echo lessens or disappears. In Adela's moment of vision at the trial, she sees her situation in both its present and its eternal aspect; and she momentarily attains wholeness. The day at the Marabar now seems one of "indescribable splendour"; and Adela pierces through to the other side of her delusion to see it truly. She achieves a doubleness of vision which enables her to see that in any fundamental sense Aziz could not be guilty of his imputed crime. She now judges Aziz for what he is, not in terms of racial prejudice.

As for Mrs. Moore, she identifies herself at first too easily with the infinite. In her "itch for the seemly," she finds it difficult to acknowledge that mystical experience can be violent rather than serene, Dionysian rather than Apollonian. As one who desires "that joy shall be graceful and sorrow august and infinity have a form" (211), she is undone by India's sheer vitality, size, and age. In contrast to Islam and Christianity, Hinduism is able to "dethrone its highest conceptions" [28] since the pursuit of the inconceivable may sometimes demand this dethronement of us. Mrs. Moore is reluctant to do so, but finds nevertheless that all great concepts—Heaven, Hell, Annihilation—deteriorate, and that "spiritual muddledom" prevails; "we can neither act nor refrain from action, we can neither ignore nor respect Infinity" (208). Mrs. Moore sneers at love ("And all this rubbish about love, love in a church, love in a cave, as if there is the least difference" [202]); but with the deepest part of her being she is faithful to this force.

On her way from India she perceives that her nihilism may have been mistaken. The palms wave to her and say the Marabar was neither final nor the echo all of India. She fails as woman until too late to see this truth; but, as a Hindu goddess after her death, she acts from the full truth which had eluded her as a woman. If Mrs. Moore had in some crises been ineffective, she is nevertheless immortal as she survives into the memory of all who knew her. She has affected the innermost nature of one man, Aziz, who hears the notes of his salvation at the trial, "Esmiss Esmoor" repeated in the interstices of the "Radhakrishna" song at the Mau festivities.

Mrs. Moore's fate in India seems similar to that of certain earlier Europeans who were more sympathetic to the Indians than most Anglo-Indians now are. For it was once possible for any mortal to become "not a whole god . . . but part of one, adding an epithet or gesture to what already existed, just as the gods contribute to the great gods, and they to the philosophic Brahm" (257). As a goddess, her influence survives in the soul of Aziz to enable him once again—through her children—to be a friend to Fielding. As she survives in Godbole's memory and becomes absorbed in the unity of the universe, he impels himself toward her mentally. She has achieved, moreover, a completion in death—in the world soul—that had evaded her in life. Her redemptive and godlike aspect has already been mentioned; and, in this aspect of her being, she is a "great mother" or "Kali" figure.[29]

And thus she is a kind of tutelary genius for the book, since through Ralph and Stella she has been able to influence Fielding and Aziz and since Adela owes so much to her. Her final effects upon the characters are convincing precisely because they have been won at such great expense, by a process involving not only regeneration but disintegration and death. Through her death, she infuses renewed life in others: she thus symbolically projects the most compelling antithesis in this multi-faceted book.

CHAPTER 6

"Unexplored Riches and Unused Methods of Release": Nonfictional Prose and General Estimate

FORSTER'S reputation rests chiefly on his novels, but his other writings are important. They make definite the ideas embedded in the novels, and they give firm expression to the liberal humanism. Some of the prose appeared before *A Passage to India,* but most of it came after this final novel. The only way he was able to comment on an unfamiliar world, he found, was through the less demanding forms of biography, the travel sketch, the personal essay, and the expository and critical treatise. Each of the volumes since 1924 has added significantly to the Forster canon, though not so boldly as another novel would have. Still, Forster's work would be less rich if he had ceased writing after 1924.

These books are important for what they reveal about Forster's ideas and intellectual preferences—and more important still for what they impart about his personality and attitudes. In short, Forster is a gifted practitioner of the personal essay, the informal sketch, and the impressionistic critique. His occasional pieces and lectures have more than transient worth, as they form the matrix of *Aspects of the Novel* (1927), *Abinger Harvest* (1936), and *Two Cheers for Democracy* (1951), books which invite us to browse for enjoyment and stimulus.

The familiar essayist's artistry, the intellectual's cultivation, the shrewd observer's penetration into the motives and the personalities of his fellow men, the poet's sensitivity to place, and the eclectic critic's identification with the achievements of another—such are the leading aspects of Forster's non-fiction. In the late 1920's and thereafter Forster wrote lucid and attractive works, less brilliant than the novels but possessing substantial worth. His toughness of spirit and his consciousness that his standards are important lend unity, weight, and even urgency to these books.

I *"At a Slight Angle to the Universe": History, Travel,*
and Biography

As a volunteer with the Red Cross in Alexandria during World
War I, Forster was impressed, he says in *Alexandria,* by "the
magic and the antiquity and the complexity of the city, and determined to write about her" (xv). In *Alexandria* (1922) and in
Pharos and Pharillon (1923) he considers the city and its denizens
of the past and present. In addition to the spell of tradition, the
colorful place and powerful personalities impart flavor to these
books. Forster's aim throughout is to capture both the outlines
and the essence of the city:

Immortal, yet somehow or other unsatisfactory, Menelaus accordingly leads the Alexandrian pageant with solid tread; cotton-brokers
conclude it: the intermediate space is thronged with phantoms,
noiseless, insubstantial, innumerable, but not without interest for the
historian. (*Pharos,* 99)

Pharos, the great lighthouse that stood for centuries at the mouth
of the Nile, brings to focus Forster's reflections upon the older
metropolis and its leaders such as Alexander, Philo, Clement, St.
Athanasius, and Arius.

More recent activities and people he presents under the rubric
"Pharillon," the "obscure" and smaller successor to Pharos. He appreciates rich personalities like the seventeenth-century traveler
Eliza Fay and the recent poet Cavafy; he depicts vividly such
varied aspects of city life as cotton-trading and drug addiction;
and he relates the topography of the present city to the old thor-
oughfares, the ancient Gates of Sun and Moon, Lake Mareotis,
and the surrounding desert. In the first section of *Alexandria,* he
sketches the history of the city and its culture more completely
than he does in *Pharos and Pharillon.*

Forster's sensitivity, luminous mind, and individual way of seeing things as he stands "at a slight angle to the universe" (*Pharos,*
92) blend to make his Egypt authentic. While neither book is
definitive history, each still has literary and stylistic distinction.
Thus Forster interprets with wit and penetration the humanizing
influence of Alexandria as she discouraged the ascetic excesses of
the early Christians: she taught that "the graciousness of Greece

[is] not quite incompatible with the Grace of God" (42). With like precision he expresses the difference between Athanasius and the less worldly Arius: Athanasius like Arius "knew what truth is, but, being a politician, he knew how truth can best be enforced" (48). In the same wise and witty manner, Forster then mocks Neo-Platonic spirituality by depicting Plotinus as a soldier, in a campaign against Persia, being "very nearly relieved of the disgrace of having a body" (*Alexandria,* 69).

In many of the writings gathered into *Abinger Harvest* and *Two Cheers for Democracy* Forster follows the course he pursued in the Alexandria books. He is fascinated by arresting personalities and by their influence on us, men like Cardan, Gemistus Pletho, Voltaire, Gibbon, Coleridge, Wilfrid Blunt, the Emperor Babur. Each of the portraits reaches beyond known fact to establish the essence of a personality as Forster sees it. The novelist's sense of idiosyncrasy and exact motive, the pungent generalization, the sympathy revealed for the varieties of personality, and the fixing of the man's relationship to the larger world—all contribute to the excitement and creative force implicit in these sketches.

Forster has been preoccupied, too, with people close to him by blood and with his maternal ancestors in particular. He writes accurately and affectionately of these forebears in his biography of the one who touched him nearest, Marianne Thornton. Affection tempers his knowledge of their defects, and respect for their virtues compensates for his candid scrutiny of their lives. He evokes the old house, Battersea Rise, not only as a bastion of privilege but as the center for a spacious mode of life and as the symbol for the Thornton steadfastness and seriousness. He appreciates Henry Thornton, the founder of the clan, for his self-sufficiency, despite his Thornton tendency to rationalize his motives by imposing on them a Christian gloss.

Forster manifests the same firmness and sympathy when he comes to the next generation and depicts for us the younger Henry and his sister Marianne, and when he traces the proliferation of the family into the later century. The subsidiary family members he brings alive with a kindred force, homage, and humor. For his total picture he gains authority by ample quoting from Marianne's letters and related documents. Aunt Marianne emerges from the past with the same tautness, the same remote-

ness and charm, that we associate with a figure in a sampler. For-
ster presented some other views of his Clapham ancestral past in
"Mrs. Hannah More" and "Battersea Rise" in *Abinger Harvest* and
"Bishop Jebb's Book" and "Henry Thornton" in *Two Cheers for
Democracy.*

Forster also wrote of people he had known intimately but who
had since died. Apparently, he wished to give some lasting form
to his impressions of them. His most extensive commemorative
work is *Goldsworthy Lowes Dickinson.* When he writes of the
years just gone, persons and places tend to merge, so that in
Goldsworthy Lowes Dickinson turn-of-the-century Cambridge is
hardly to be dissociated from the people, especially Dickinson and
Nathaniel Wedd, who had meant most to him there. This feeling
for place and this evocation of the recent past (the World War I
milieu, especially, in which Dickinson achieved some authority
with his concept of a League of Nations) endow with immediacy
a personality unexciting except to those who knew him well. For
what it reveals about Forster more than for what it says about
Dickinson the book is indispensable. The commemorative impulse
also led to incidental studies of "Roger Fry," "Forrest Reid,"
"Howard Overing Sturgis," and "T. E. Lawrence" in *Abinger Harvest* and of "Edward Carpenter" and "Webb and Webb" in *Two
Cheers for Democracy.*

Just as in his fiction Forster captures the savor and complexity
of a whole civilization—English, Italian, or Indian—so does he in
some of his best incidental prose. Preeminent are his writings on
India: *The Hill of Devi* and some of the essays in *Abinger Harvest.* Forster's own life in India and his immediate reactions to it
comprise *The Hill of Devi.* As in *A Passage to India,* Forster com-
municates a sense of a sprawling continent bursting with life but
baffling our full comprehension. His grasp of the involutions of
character enables him to re-create forcibly such dignitaries, British and Indian, as Malcolm Darling (tutor to the Bapu Sahib),
Josie (his warm-hearted wife), Colonel Wilson (the paranoid
civil servant who maligned Forster), the Maharajah of Chhatar-
pur, Bapu Sahib (the Maharajah of Dewas Senior), the Dowa-
ger Maharini (his contentious aunt), and Scindhia (the Maharajah of Gwalior and the vulgar uncle of Bapu Sahib). Bapu Sahib
stands with Forster's other extended portraits of Indians in *A Pas-*

sage to India; an all too fallible saint, he lingers in the mind with all his contradictions much as do Aziz and Godbole.

For the purpose of creating verisimilitude, Forster uses copiously his own letters, diaries, and reminiscences in *The Hill of Devi.* But these are not ordinary documents since Forster's talent is such that in all his descriptive prose he appeals subtly to our senses and imagination. He helps us thereby to grasp the full life of an alien civilization, its surface aspects and its deeper implications. He reveals, moreover, as he did in *A Passage to India,* some of the disparities existing between the culture of the Orient and the British sensibility. He recurs to this contrast between Occident and Orient and the need for mutual understanding in such important essays in *Abinger Harvest* as "Salute to the Orient," "The Mind of the Indian Native State," and "Adrift in India." The India which Forster embraced in novel and travel book alike claims our attention principally as a culture important in its own right. Like the writings on India, "Clouds Hill" (T. E. Lawrence's home in Dorset), "London Is a Muddle," and "Cambridge" of *Two Cheers for Democracy* again reflect, and gain impressiveness from, Forster's sensitivity to milieu.

II *"A World of . . . Richness and Subtlety": Personal, Political, and Social Commentary*

Personal, political, and social commentary is diffused among Forster's books. Some of his best essays develop his views on the relationships that prevail, or ought to prevail, among human beings. The best known, "What I Believe" (*Two Cheers*) is Forster's fullest statement of his humanism, with its stress on values personal, intellectual, and tentative in kind. This "confession" gains distinction less from the originality of the ideas than from the sincerity with which they are expressed. Other essays as well from *Two Cheers for Democracy* weld the personal and the political. In "Three Anti-Nazi Broadcasts," "The Menace to Freedom," and "Racial Exercise," Forster evinces vehement emotion and an uncompromising opposition to intellectual and political tyranny. In one frame of mind, Forster felt despair almost overwhelm him as he viewed the approaching cataclysm of war ("Post Munich" and "They Hold Their Tongues"). In another, a qualified hopefulness gains ascendancy ("Tolerance," "The Challenge of Our

Time," "George Orwell," and "The Tercentenary of the 'Areopagitica' ").

Forster was less involved politically and socially in the earlier *Abinger Harvest*. Characteristically, the social commentary in it centers on English society itself, its distinctive traits, limitations, and tentative virtues. "Notes on the English Character," with its analysis of middle-class strengths and hypocrisies, is analytical and, in direction, negative: there is more to be corrected in England than to congratulate it on. All too often, Englishmen go forth from public school "into a world of whose richness and subtlety they have no conception." In contrast, "Liberty in England" (1935) notes that, for all its defects, English civilization has always been the guardian of liberty. Satire predominates in "Mrs. Grundy at the Parkers" (which exposes British moral hypocrisy); "Me, Them and You" (which excoriates public indifference to the sacrifices made by soldiers in the war); and "The Birth of an Empire" (which lightly scrutinizes British imperialism). Some of the best essays in *Abinger Harvest* approach modern life from the point of view of the detached moralist: "My Wood" distinguishes an acceptable materialism and carnality from an unacceptable, and "Our Diversions" analyzes the merits and deficiencies of popular culture. Always Forster is persuasive as a social commentator because he is urbane and reserved, yet personal and intelligent.

III   *"Applying Logic to the Illogical": Literary Criticism*

Of greater importance than these commentaries are Forster's essays on literature and writers. Apparently, he came to theory and esthetics late. A few early efforts in *Abinger Harvest* reveal incidental concern with literary theory; and "Anonymity: an Enquiry" dates from 1925, though it is collected in *Two Cheers for Democracy*. As literary critic Forster is best known for *Aspects of the Novel* (1927), now one of the standard books on narrative, despite its being somewhat tentative in method and in the conclusions reached. Forster has not only provided us with terms of discourse for the novel (he divides his book into "The Story," "People," "The Plot," "Fantasy," "Prophesy," and "Pattern and Rhythm"), but he writes as one who loves literature. He reveals firmness of mind and depth of sensibility; he understands, moreover, the novelist's practice and the problems associated with creativity.

Forster's views on theory and his specific judgments are alike stimulating. He sees the fundamental tension in the novel as that between "life in time" and "the life by values." The life by values the writer expresses through his temperament. As the revelation, then, of the author's view of the world, the novel is to be differentiated from history which, like the novel, finds chronology to be indispensable. The novelist, more concerned with people as such, penetrates farther into their hidden lives than does the historian. For Forster, pattern is less important than energy, even when such energy is less than perfectly articulated. Skilled management of point of view, for example, provides less authentic life for the novel than "a proper mixture of characters." As for plot, it seeks the causal connections between events rather than their temporal progression. Curiosity is gratified by its means, as "the memory of the reader ('that dull glow of the mind of which intelligence is the bright advancing edge')" (88) helps shape the book in his mind. Some of Forster's other concepts, especially those found in "Fantasy," "Prophesy," and "Pattern and Rhythm," I have referred to previously.

Forster is excellent on individual books and authors. He views Hardy as a writer "who conceives of his novels from an enormous height" (93); he sees James as a master at envisioning the "second-rate" character ("deficient in sensitiveness, abounding in the wrong sort of worldliness" [157]); he praises Meredith as one who achieves unerring balance between character and the requirements of plot (the concealment of Letitia Dale's changed attitude in *The Egoist* is a great triumph); and he regards Jane Austen as a major novelist because her "characters are ready for an extended life, for a life which the scheme of her books seldom requires them to lead" (75). He cites "the charmed stagnation" of Sterne's *Tristram Shandy*, he notes the immensities of space in *War and Peace* and how they generate intensity and mute Tolstoy's pessimism, and he observes in Beerbohm's *Zuleika Dobson* the "criticisms of human nature [which] fly through the book, not like arrows but upon the wings of sylphs" (118).

Most of Forster's theorizing came in the 1930's and the 1940's. Only late in life, apparently, did Forster make conscious (though not systematic) attempts to formulate the views of art and literature on which he had acted for thirty years or more. Perhaps he did not systematize his ideas sooner because they are not numerous, strikingly original, or rigidly adhered to. He is primarily a subjective, impressionistic critic who tries to identify with an author rather than judge books or approach a writer through literary history.

Regarding literary art, Forster as critic faces two ways. He distrusts analytic discourse because it comes between literature and the reader, but he values the intelligence as it clarifies and makes more available a master work. The critic's task is endless, he says in *Abinger Harvest,* since it consists of "applying logic to the illogical" (40). Criticism helps the artist only minimally: in great matters, his own discernment can alone serve him. But the sophisticated critic can encourage the reader or spectator to know the world of the senses and to sharpen his reactions to it. Criticism can also help "civilize the community" and expose the fraudulent and pretentious. The conscientious critic reveals sympathy with detachment, a ranging imagination, and a wide perspective.

Reflecting the organic view of literature embraced by the Romantics, Forster regards each creation as a self-contained entity in which whole and part are closely fused. He stresses also the internal coherence that is characteristic of the notable work of art. Order results from the active imagination of the artist who impresses his sensibility on all parts of his creation. The writer must be attentive not only to form but to style, for the smaller as well as the larger components of a work acquire intensity to the degree that his sensibility confronts them.

Forster, who espouses a paradoxical view of art, views it as self-contained even while its influence radiates beyond its demarcated universe. Art is at once esthetic and ethical in nature and authority, at once individual and social in origin and significance. The greater the artist, the more complete is his response to the complexities of life and the more inclusive is his vision. In any case, his work bridges the realm of the mind and the empirically perceived world without. He is a realist to the degree that he uses the outer world as basis for his creations but an antirealist to the extent that he captures the symbolical and the transcendent implications in his experience.

In practice Forster combines elucidation of texts and consideration of the artist's general tendencies. Elaborate analysis of individual works is infrequent; but in some of his later critiques— "The Ascent of F-6," "John Skelton," "George Crabbe and Peter

Grimes," and "Virginia Woolf"—he concentrates with insight on single books or poems. In most of the essays he prefers to consider the writer's canon and to explain its leading characteristics.

Forster's best critical pieces, though impressionistic in tone and manner, develop the generalities he derives from examining the corpus of a writer's work. He finds, accordingly, that a "primeval romanticism" explains more about Ibsen's dramas than any other principle; he sees a horror in T. S. Eliot's earlier work so intense that the poet cannot always express it clearly; and he notes in Proust how both curiosity and despair determine the tone and texture of his "epic of decay." In "The Early Novels of Virginia Woolf," Forster asserts that Mrs. Woolf elevates sensation to an esthetic principle while she re-creates the physical processes of thought more convincingly than any other novelist has. In "Sinclair Lewis" Forster sees the novelist after a short while as limited by a photographic use of detail, in "T. E. Lawrence" he discovers in the *Seven Pillars of Wisdom* a monumental record not so much of a great undertaking as of a complex personality, in "John Skelton" he finds a satirist whose bitterness is balanced by fearlessness, and in "George Crabbe and Peter Grimes" he observes a large-souled man overcoming his revulsion from the meanness of East Anglian rural life.

Though Forster develops guiding ideas in examining a writer, he chiefly conveys the essential aspects of an author or an important work through the vivid phrase or succinct statement. His impression, recorded in *Abinger Harvest*, of Septimus Smith in relation to Mrs. Woolf's heroine in *Mrs. Dalloway* is incisive: "His foot has slipped through the gay surface on which she still stands —that is all the difference between them" (111). Then, with *A Remembrance of Things Past*, Forster conveys in *Two Cheers for Democracy* the substance of this *roman fleuve* while he appositely describes it:

. . . it is full of echoes, exquisite reminders, intelligent parallels, which delight the attentive reader, and at the end, and not until the end, he realises that those echoes and parallels occur as it were inside a gigantic cathedral; that the book, which seemed as we read it so rambling, has an architectural unity and pre-ordained form. (224)

IV *"Beauty at Which a Novelist Should Never Aim":*
   Forster and the Art of the Novel

Forster has been censured by some critics for the plots of his
novels, for an excess of contrivance, an overuse of surprise, and a
resort to melodrama. Others have felt that the direction of the
action is arbitrarily determined and that the free development of
the characters is thereby inhibited. Such judgments stem from
standards ordinarily applied to realistic novels, standards that are
appropriate in part to Forster's fiction since much of it is rooted in
social comedy and moral speculation. He defines his own method
perhaps in defining Virginia Woolf's in *Abinger Harvest.* She
goes, as he does, from fact to its final significance: "Required like
most writers to choose between the surface and the depths as the
basis of her operations, she chooses the surface and then burrows
in as far as she can" (111). But, if Forster has some sense of the
empiric verities, he does not stop short at them in his narratives.

Ultimately, he wishes to communicate his subjective and ecstatic vision of reality, the result in large part of his intense Romanticism of temper. The emotional and transcendent impact of
what he creates is for him more arresting than its analytic implications. Thus, the facts of perception and the motives underlying
action pale before his compulsion to relate them to his intuitive
and mystical insights. This realm of the extrasensory overlays the
social milieu that Forster knows as insider and is intricately inter-
twined with it; but as it reflects an eternal order of value, this
extrasensory realm is also independent of such milieu. Leavis,
who is unsympathetic to this side of Forster, nevertheless perceives why he rejected the realistic as basis for any final truth.
Forster, Leavis says (262), was preoccupied with vitality to the
extent that he inevitably went beyond social comedy to the prov-
ince of poetry.

Forster is not so careless with plot as some readers have
thought. He is only partly a Realistic novelist and uses plot to
achieve effects other than the establishing of verisimilitude. He
is—and perhaps basically—a fabulist or romancer or prophet, as
George H. Thomson has so convincingly demonstrated in *The
Fiction of E. M. Forster.* As such, Forster dramatizes, in intricate
fictions, his conceptions of the complexities of the human situation, not only as it appears in the here and now but under the

aspect of eternity. As a result, certain of his characters become heightened or foreshortened as they help articulate his vision; and they become symbols as they dramatize his intuitive realizations. As John Crowe Ransom has said, Forster surpasses others of the Liberal school by this sheer susceptibility to the ineffable, by "his fertility in ascribing aesthetic vision to the consciousness of his pet characters; or for that matter, the reception of the vision into his own consciousness, whenever the occasion rises, which is eternally." [1]

In the tradition of romance with its archetypal figures, Forster's books contain major characters that are often more arresting as felt presences than for the social relationships they exemplify. On occasion, Forster designedly sacrifices probability of motive in the interests of ulterior truth. Characters like Gino Carella, Stephen Wonham, and Ruth Wilcox lack sufficient substance as real people to be entirely convincing, yet as presences they are not the esthetic failures that some critics have declared them to be. What each lacks for our complete suspension of disbelief in him is not added consistency in motivation but a completer conception on Forster's part of him and of his role in the given book.

As fabulist, romancer, and prophet, Forster has evolved complex plots which are, nevertheless, consistent within themselves and which communicate his intuitions more forcibly than would actions of greater moment and probability. The alternation of the idyllic and the violent, for example, establishes more vividly Forster's sense of the disjunctions in experience than would a more consecutive recounting of event. Such disjunctions achieve, moreover, some resolution in a timeless entity extending beyond our ordinary lives in time, since Forster, as we have seen, is a mediator of extremes and something of a mystic as well.

Forster once declared to Angus Wilson that theme in part determined the incidents. These are truly important, then, as they relate to theme; as they illustrate the inner tensions of the characters, their relationships to each other, and their aspirations; and as they embody the symbolic implications of the fable. Characters, insofar as they embody theme, must in some part have also antedated story line as Forster shaped his fiction; and, like the incidents of the plot, they readily attain general, symbolic dimensions.

Forster's characters, then, are often less significant in themselves than for what they suggest as we review the narratives. Except for the "flat" characters—like most of the Indians and Anglo-Indians in *A Passage to India,* Mrs. Lewin in *The Longest Journey,* and Mrs. Munt and Frieda Mosebach in *Howards End*— the characters have an allegorical aspect in the novels which varies in complexity from the crass Philistinism of Paul Wilcox in *Howards End* to the complicated humanism and transcendental sensitivity of Margaret Schlegel. His best creations—Philip Herriton, Caroline Abbott, Cecil Vyse, Lucy Honeychurch, the Schlegel sisters, Henry Wilcox, Rickie Elliot, Stewart Ansell, Agnes Pembroke, Aziz, Mrs. Moore, Adela Quested, Fielding, and Godbole—are not only significant as recognizable human beings facing recognizable human difficulties but as participants in Forster's totally envisioned panorama of human activity. Although most of his figures have this enlarged aspect, I think that Thomson is right in judging that only certain characters, those awake to the visionary, are truly archetypal.[2]

More than the characters, some of the incidents—and even the objects—of Forster's novels gather a symbolic, often a supernal, aura as they bring to focus the ineffable truths which Forster wishes to communicate. Incidents and objects become more compelling for what they imply in the full design of the work than for what they literally signify. The dynamic quality of Forster's symbolism depends more on the fact that his characters and actions simultaneously face toward the actual and the ineffable than on the repetition of images and the heightening of style. Forster does not always achieve the fusion of social reality and transcendental value for which he strives, but the fusion is more adroit and the symbolism more organic to total structure than critics like Leavis and Walter Allen admit.

But, if artistry is not solely a function of Forster's use of rhythm (in the sense of repeated phrases and images) and the presence of a luminous and evocative style, these elements are still integral to his achievement. If the characters are typically caught between the worlds of the actual and the transcendent, if they reveal their ability or incapacity to mediate between these worlds, and if incident provides philosophic commentary upon the characters, still, in *A Passage to India,* for example, such images as the "fists and fingers" of the Marabar Caves, the receding arches in mosque and sky, and the natural phenomena such as stone, fire, rain, and the parched earth all help generate the book's density.

And it is the style that gives Forster's fiction—and his non-fiction as well—its freshness, individuality, and resonance. Almost any page illustrates the beauty and originality of the style but this passage, depicting Leonard Bast and his journey from London to Howards End, is typical:

Tunnels followed, and after each the sky grew bluer, and from the embankment at Finsbury Park he had his first sight of the sun. It rolled along behind the eastern smokes—a wheel, whose fellow was the descending moon—and as yet it seemed the servant of the blue sky, not its lord. He dozed again. Over Tewin Water it was day. To the left fell the shadow of the embankment and its arches; to the right Leonard saw up into the Tewin Woods and towards the church, with its wild legend of immortality. Six forest trees—that is a fact—grow out of one of the graves in Tewin churchyard. The grave's occupant—that is the legend—is an atheist, who declared that if God existed, six forest trees would grow out of her grave. These things in Hertfordshire; and farther afield lay the house of a hermit—Mrs. Wilcox had known him—who barred himself up, and wrote prophecies, and gave all he had to the poor. While, powdered in between, were the villas of business men, who saw life more steadily, though with the steadiness of the half-closed eye. Over all the sun was streaming, to all the birds were singing, to all the primroses were yellow, and the speedwell blue, and the country, however they interpreted her, was uttering her cry of "now." She did not free Leonard yet, and the knife plunged deeper into his heart as the train drew up at Hilton. But remorse had become beautiful. (322–23)

We may note, first, the element of the specific—the fact that Forster is describing an actual countryside where places have actual names. He evokes sun, sky, and flowers to the senses, and thereby gains credence for the touch of fantasy surrounding Tewin Church. He not only modulates from concreteness to fantasy but from Leonard's point of view to the omniscient author's. Scene and individual interact as Leonard, in spite of his depression, goes from apathy to appreciation of its beauties. One aspect of Forster's deftness as artist is just this ability to objectify the subjective thoughts of an individual by relating them to the people and objects about him. Through indirection but always concretely, he is able to convey, furthermore, the evanescent, intangible aspects of personality and the individual's inner life.

Sensitivity to light and shadow accounts in part for Forster's luminous prose. The reactions to physical impressions are so heightened that Forster conveys through their means an impression that the physical and spiritual are parts of each other, that the streaming lights of nature and the visionary gleams in the soul share reality as parts of a divine entity which we can only intermittently apprehend. In a passage such as the one just quoted, exact observation, supple sensibility, imaginative power, and spiritual exaltation blend to create an authentic poetry in prose.

But the passage reveals intellectual rigor and a subtle mind. There is incisiveness and astringency when the narrator (or Forster), mentioning the rural villas, scorns their businessmen owners as seeing life "with the steadiness of the half-closed eye." Most of the author comment comes in such controlled form, and it elucidates rather than interrupts action and psychology. As Forster regulates tone in observations of this kind, he is able to present matters of portent with a detached, ironic perspective, and to suggest, through oblique means, intuitions more profound than he could through unmodulated comment. The irony and understatement, the pointed observation and the restrained expression, combine to make the ideas functional rather than intrusive. The aphorisms actually move the novel forward and elucidate character, incident, and value; and they are at least partly organic to the novel's life and structure.

Some statements are, however, memorable in themselves, as this brief sampling from *Howards End* may indicate:

One death may explain itself, but it throws no light upon another: the groping inquiry must begin anew. Preachers or scientists may generalize, but we know that no generality is possible about those whom we love; not one heaven awaits them, not even one oblivion. (276)

. . . .

Were they normal? What a question to ask! And it is always those who know nothing about human nature, who are bored by psychology and shocked by physiology, who ask it. (288–89)

. . . .

Remorse is not among the eternal verities. . . . And of all the means to regeneration, Remorse is surely the most wasteful. It cuts away healthy tissues with the poisoned. It is a knife that probes far deeper than the evil. (316)

Through statement, style, sensibility, and an active imagination, Forster's own personality and values suffuse his fiction. He approximates, in short, his own conception, expressed in *Aspects of the Novel*, of the perfect novelist as one "who touches all his material directly, who seems to pass the creative finger down every sentence and into every word" (72). Such a novelist's work becomes then a manifestation of his own geniality and passion, a reflection of his own lucid intelligence and his visionary intensity.

His personality and values are positive in their implications despite his realization of human imperfections and the tragedy of unfulfilled aspirations. In 1951 Forster could say that "human life is" still active, still carrying about with it unexplored riches and unused methods of release" (*Two Cheers*, xii). It is just this sense of the inexhaustible nature of human powers that gives his pages their reach and spiritual abundance. The acute intellect and mature sensibility that we find in Forster, he himself finds in Ibsen, "the romantic."

The interpenetrations between the solid world of society and the intangible realm of spirit provide focus for Ibsen's art, just as they characterize Forster's own. Both men work inward to the essence of their perceptions and to a realization of their unexpected relationships. What Forster observes of Ibsen's art in *Abinger Harvest* applies as surely to his own:

To his impassioned vision dead and damaged things, however contemptible socially, dwell for ever in the land of romance, and this is the secret of his so-called symbolism: a connection is found between objects that lead different types of existence; they reinforce one another and each lives more intensely than before. Consequently his stage throbs with a mysteriousness for which no obvious preparation has been made, with beckonings, tremblings, sudden compressions of the air, and his characters as they wrangle among the oval tables and stoves are watched by an unseen power which slips between their words. (86)

In Ibsen there is, besides, the fine balance between feeling and detachment which Forster found remarkable in Wilfrid Blunt, for instance, and which, of course, he himself exemplifies.

In his novels and miscellaneous books alike, Forster's aim is to shape refractory experience to the requirements of order and pattern, but not at the expense of its vitality or of the intensity of his vision. He achieves harmony and shapeliness in his fiction, qualities he suspects in writers like Henry James and André Gide who seek too avidly for satisfaction in technique and structure. Still, his own work emanates from that residual sensitivity to esthetic forms and impressions which the truly creative novelist must, for Forster, possess. In a general discussion in *Aspects of the Novel*, he asserts that such sensitivity results in a beauty which we as readers find amply revealed in Forster's own works, that "beauty at which a novelist should never aim, though he fails if he does not achieve it" (88). He has, moreover, the faith, possessed by the Romantics, in the transforming aspects of the imagination, "the immortal God which should assume flesh for the redemption of mortal passion" (*Two Cheers,* 88). The creative imagination breathes through all his work and gives it incandescence whatever its flaws may be.

If Forster lacks breadth, he is always fresh, personal, and original—often profound and deeply moving. The fascination exerted by characters who grip our minds; the wit and beauty present in the always limpid style; a passionate involvement with life in all its variety; a view of existence alive to its comic incongruities and to its tragic implications; and a steady adherence to humanistic values which compel admiration even if their entire relevance may sometimes be in question—such are the leading aspects of Forster's work that have lured modern readers to it. As the recent critical interest in it signifies, they have been convinced of its excellence and confirmed in their impression of Forster's absolute worth as critical intelligence and as novelist.

Notes and References

Preface

1. *Books and Persons* (New York, 1917), p. 293.
2. Samuel Hynes, "Forster at Eighty-Five: The Old Man at King's," *Commonweal*, LXXIX (February 21, 1964), 635–38.
3. David Jones, "E. M. Forster on His Life and His Books," *Listener*, LXI (January 1, 1959), 11–12.

Chapter One

1. "The Long Run," *New Statesman and Nation*, n. s. XVI (December 10, 1938), 971.
2. See Frederick C. Crews, *E. M. Forster: The Perils of Humanism* (Princeton, 1962), chap. i–v and Wilfred Stone, *The Cave and the Mountain: A Study of E. M. Forster* (Stanford, 1966), chap. ii.
3. For slightly varying accounts of Bloomsbury and its origins, consult Crews, 42–49; William Van O'Connor, "Toward a History of Bloomsbury," *Southwest Review*, XL (Winter, 1955), 35–62; Clive Bell, *Old Friends* (New York, 1956), pp. 25–28, 126–37; Leonard Woolf, *Beginning Again* (London, 1964), pp. 22–26, and *Downhill All the Way* (London, 1967), pp. 114–15; Noel Annan, *Leslie Stephen* (Cambridge, Mass., 1952), p. 123; J. K. Johnstone, *The Bloomsbury Group* (New York, 1954); Michael Holroyd, *Lytton Strachey*, 2 vols. (New York, 1968); and Quentin Bell, *Bloomsbury* (London, 1968).
4. "Culture and Freedom," *Two Cheers*, 35; "What I Believe," 67; *Alexandria*, 78.
5. Harvey Breit, *The Writer Observed* (Cleveland, 1956), p. 55.
6. "Equality," *Mixed Essays* (1879); reprinted in Lionel Trilling (ed.), *The Portable Matthew Arnold* (New York, 1949).
7. "Notes for a Reply," in *Julian Bell, Essays, Poems and Letters*, ed. Quentin Bell (London, 1938), p. 391.
8. "The Individual and His God," *Listener*, XXIV (December 5, 1940), 802.
9. For a perceptive discussion of this subject, see Edwin Nierenberg, "The Prophecy of E. M. Forster," *Queen's Quarterly*, LXXI (1964), 189–202.

10. "Foreword" (London, 1927).

11. "A Great History," *Athenaeum* (July 9, 1920), 42–43.

12. *Rage for Order* (Chicago, 1948), p. 132.

13. "Introduction," *The Longest Journey* (World's Classics Edition), p. ix.

14. *Nation* (London), XXXVII (August 8, 1925), 568–69.

15. "That Job's Done," *Listener*, XVII (March 10, 1937), supplement iv.

16. "An Indian on W. B. Yeats," *Listener*, XXIX (December 24, 1942), 824.

17. "Introduction," *Lord of the Flies* (New York, 1962), p. x.

18. See H. A. Smith, "Forster's Humanism and the Nineteenth Century," in *Forster: A Collection of Critical Essays*, ed. Malcolm Bradbury (Englewood Cliffs, 1966).

19. "Preface," Dickinson, *The Greek View of Life* (London, 23rd ed.; 1957), p. vi.

20. "Dante," *Working Men's College Journal*, X (April, 1908), 302.

21. "English Freedom," *Spectator*, CLII (November 23, 1934), 792.

22. "Jehovah, Buddha and the Greeks," *Athenaeum* (June 4, 1920), 730.

23. "William Cowper, An Englishman," *Spectator*, CXLVIII (January 16, 1932), 75.

24. "English Freedom," 792.

25. "The Prince's Tale," *Spectator*, CCIV (May 13, 1960), 702; "Introduction," Giuseppi di Lampedusa, *Two Stories and a Memory* (New York, 1962), p. 16.

26. " 'In the Rue Lepsius,' " *Listener*, XLVI (July 5, 1951), 29.

27. "Consolations of History" in *Abinger Harvest;* "Recollectionism" in *New Statesman and Nation*, n.s., XIII (March 13, 1937), 405–6.

28. "Some Memories," *Edward Carpenter: In Appreciation*, ed. Gilbert Beith (London, 1931), p. 76.

29. "More Browning Letters," *Listener*, XVIII (October 13, 1937), supplement xv.

30. "A Clash of Authority," *Listener*, XXXI (June 22), 686.

31. "Tolerance" (*Two Cheers*, 45); "The Unsung Virtue of Tolerance," *Listener*, XXVI (July 31, 1941), 160.

32. "Toward a Definition of Tolerance," *New York Times Magazine* (February 22, 1953), 13.

33. "Ibsen the Romantic," *Nation and Athenaeum* (March 17, 1928), 903.

34. "Indian Entries from a Diary," *Harper's Magazine*, CCXXIV (February, 1962), 51.

35. "William Cowper," 75.

36. "The Long Run," 970–72.

37. "Notes on the Way," *Time and Tide*, XVI (November 23, 1935), 1703–4; see also *Two Cheers*, 25–27.

38. "The Ivory Tower," *Atlantic Monthly*, CLXIII (January, 1939), 51–58.

39. "A Conversation," *Spectator*, CLIX (August 13, 1937), 269–270; "Notes on the Way," *Time and Tide*, XVI (November 2, 1935), 1572.

40. "The University and the Universe," *Spectator*, CL (March 17, 1933), 368–69.

41. See note 38.

42. See Herbert Haworth, "E. M. Forster and the Contrite Establishment," *Journal of General Education*, XVII (1965), 196–206.

43. "Notes on Egypt," *The Government of Egypt* (London, 1920); letter, *Times* (London), November 13, 1919, p. 8, on British exploitation of Egyptian laborers; and essays in Part IV, *Abinger Harvest*.

44. "The Censorship of Books," *Nineteenth Century*, CV (April, 1929), 444–45; "The Freedom of the B.B.C.," *New Statesman and Nation*, n.s., I (April 4, 1931), 209–10; "The Tercentenary of the 'Areopagitica' " (1944, *Two Cheers*).

45. "Me, Them and You" (1925, *Abinger Harvest*); "The Challenge of Our Time" (1946, *Two Cheers*).

46. "Liberty in England" (1935, *Abinger Harvest*); "Still the Sedition Bill," *Time and Tide*, XV (October 27, 1934), 1340.

47. "Notes on the Way," *Time and Tide*, XV (June 16, 1934), 765–67.

48. "English Freedom," 791–92.

49. "Notes on the Way," *Time and Tide*, XV (June 2, 1934), 694–96; XVI (November 2 and 23, 1935), 1571–72, 1703–4.

50. "Jew-Consciousness" and "Racial Exercise," both 1939, *Two Cheers*. Other essays cited in this paragraph are also in *Two Cheers*.

51. "Liberty in England" (1935, *Abinger Harvest*); "International Congress of Writers," *New Statesman and Nation*, n.s., X (July 6, 1935), 9; "The Long Run," 971–72.

52. See letters to *Times* (London), October 4, 1957, p. 11; October 29, 1957, p. 11; February 19, 1958, p. 9; May 9, 1958, p. 13; October 31, 1958, p. 7; March 31, 1961, p. 15; January 2, 1962, p. 9; letter, *Spectator*, CCIX (November 30, 1962), 856.

53. "Freedom for What," *Listener*, XXI (June 1, 1939), 1177.

54. *Listener*, XXXVIII (December 11), 1029.

55. "Exercises in Perspective: Notes on the Use of Coincidence in the Novels of E. M. Forster," *Chimera*, III (Summer, 1945), 3–14.

56. "Affable Hawk," *Spectator*, CLXIX (July 23, 1932), 125.

57. "Introduction," *Lord of the Flies*, p. xi.

58. "Ancient and Modern," *Listener*, XVI (November 11, 1936), 921–22.

59. "A Letter," *Twentieth Century*, CLVII (February, 1955), 99–101; "Introduction," *Lord of the Flies*, pp. ix–xiii.

60. "Ghosts Ancient and Modern," *Spectator*, CXLVII (November 21, 1931), 672.

61. "The Charm and Strength of Mrs. Gaskell," *Sunday Times*, April 7, 1957, p. 10.

62. K. Natwar-Singh (ed.), *E. M. Forster: A Tribute* (New York, 1964), p. 73.

63. Letter, *Griffin* (1951), pp. 4–6.

Chapter Two

1. P. N. Furbank and F. J. H. Haskell, *Writers at Work*, ed. Malcolm Cowley (New York, 1958), p. 32.

2. See for instance James McConkey, *The Novels of E. M. Forster* (Ithaca, 1957), p. 102, and Frederick R. Karl and Marvin Magalaner, *A Reader's Guide to Great Twentieth Century English Novels* (New York, 1959), p. 111.

3. K. W. Gransden, *E. M. Forster* (New York, 1962), p. 28.

4. Imagery drawn from music and painting is discussed more exhaustively in J. B. Beer, *The Achievement of E. M. Forster* (New York, 1962), pp. 55 ff.

5. " 'My Poultry Are Not Officers,' " *Listener*, XXII (October 26, 1939), supplement iii.

6. For a more favorable evaluation of "The Machine Stops," see Stone, 152 ff. I discuss almost all the stories more fully in "Forster's 'Natural Supernaturalism': The Tales," *Modern Fiction Studies*, VII (1961), 271–83.

7. For a more positive interpretation than mine, see Alan Wilde, *Art and Order: A Study of E. M. Forster* (New York, 1964), pp. 92–95. For negative interpretations of Miss Raby as a proud and overbearing woman, see Stone, 137–44; and John V. Hagopian, "Eternal Moments in the Short Fiction of E. M. Forster," *College English*, XXVII (1965), 209–14.

8. "Introduction," Lampedusa, *Two Stories and a Memory*, p. 15. I no longer regard the siren as being in part a projection of moral evil; I now agree with the interpretations of Nierenberg; George H. Thomson, *The Fiction of E. M. Forster* (Detroit, 1967), pp. 84 ff.; and James L. Missey, "Forster's Redemptive Siren," *Modern Fiction Studies*, X (Winter, 1964–65), 383–85.

Chapter Three

1. "Songs of Loveliness," *Daily News* (January 27, 1920), 5.
2. "Ritual Aspects of E. M. Forster's *The Longest Journey*," *Modern Fiction Studies*, XIII (1967), 201.
3. Rex Warner, *E. M. Forster* (rev. ed.; London, 1960), p. 19.
4. See, for example, Walter Allen, *The English Novel* (New York, 1955), p. 45; Johnstone, 188; McConkey, 68; H. J. Oliver, *The Art of E. M. Forster* (Melbourne, 1960), p. 37; and Wilde, 43.

Chapter Four

1. Stone is an exception. He focuses too intently, I think, on the weaknesses and inconsistencies of the characters. The quotation from Bradbury's article, "E. M. Forster's *Howards End*," is from its revised form in Bradbury, ed., *Forster: A Collection of Critical Essays* (Englewood Cliffs, 1966), p. 130. The later quotation in my discussion has not been so revised.
2. See Edwin M. Moseley, "A New Correlative for *Howards End*: Demeter and Persephone," *Loch Haven Bulletin*, Series I, No. 3 (1961); and Forster's "Cnidus" (*Abinger Harvest*, 165–69).
3. For contrasting views, see Wilde, 119; and Thomas Churchill, "Place and Personality in *Howards End*," *Critique*, V (1962), 61–73.
4. Karl and Magalaner, 113.
5. E. B. C. Jones, *The English Novelists* (London, 1936), p. 273, ed. Derek Verschoyle.
6. This is substantially Trilling's estimate, 121. Barbara Hardy in *The Appropriate Form* (London, 1964), p. 75, feels that Ruth Wilcox fails both as a real person and as a symbolic presence. Churchill argues for her complete centrality and credibility.
7. See Rose Macaulay, *The Writings of E. M. Forster* (London, 1938), p. 113; Oliver, 46; David Cecil, *Poets and Story Tellers* (New York, 1949), p. 195.
8. Most recent critics agree with Forster except Cox and Churchill; earlier critics such as Walter Allen ("Reassessments—*Howards End*"), Savage, Tindall (*Forces in Modern British Literature*), and Swinnerton contest his reality and adequacy.
9. Wilde, 114, best analyzes Margaret's reasons for marrying Henry Wilcox.

Chapter Five

1. The book has been exhaustively studied. Accounts which have most influenced me are those by McConkey, Gransden, Thomson, Dauner, Horowitz, and Stone.
2. "The Charm and Strength of Mrs. Gaskell," 10.

3. Natwar-Singh, 50.
4. "The Gods of India," *New Weekly*, I (May 30, 1914), 338.
5. "The World Mountain," *Listener*, LII (December 2, 1954), 978.
6. "The Age of Misery," *New Weekly*, II (June 27, 1914), 52.
7. I differ here with Austin, Horowitz, and Pederson who regard Mrs. Moore as the central animating influence in the novel. I also disagree with Beer, 146, when he asserts that Godbole cannot "cope with the intractibility of the caves." He copes with it by seeing it for what it is.
8. "The Temple," *Athenaeum* (September 26, 1919), 947.
9. Natwar-Singh, xii.
10. *A Passage to India* (Everyman's ed.; London, 1942), p. xxi.
11. "The Blue Boy," *Listener*, XXII (March 14, 1957), 444; "A Great Anglo-Indian," *Daily News and Leader*, March 29, 1915, p. 7.
12. "Indian Entries from a Diary," 51.
13. All commentators agree that the caves are central to the novel. Pessimistic interpreters of the novel, with whom I disagree (Crews, Wilde, Brower), maintain that the negations embodied in the caves are never neutralized, whereas the critics mentioned in Note 1 above all feel that the caves represent only the negative pole of reality, at times an overwhelming aspect of experience but still a partial one. Wilde's statement is too extreme: "Beneath all human efforts to give form to the world, to create civilization, lies, as the novel increasingly shows, nothing—no god, no first mover, no sustaining force" (130).
14. Attempts to identify the caves with evil exclusively or otherwise to restrict their meaning (as Glen O. Allen does in identifying them with the intelligence) are, I think, oversimplifications.
15. "The Churning of the Ocean," *Athenaeum* (May 21, 1920), pp. 667–68.
16. Knowledge of God is intermittent rather than "unavailable," as Crews, 70, asserts. The presence of God can at times be felt, although He may be indifferent to any given individual's fortunes.
17. Louise Dauner in "What Happened in the Cave? Reflections on *A Passage to India*," *Modern Fiction Studies*, VII (1961), summarizes perceptively the "polyvalent" cave.
18. See especially accounts of the novel by Glen O. Allen, Dauner, Horowitz, McConkey, Moseley, and Stone.
19. Angus Wilson, "A Conversation with E. M. Forster," *Encounter*, IX (November, 1957), 54.
20. "The Art and Architecture of India," *Listener*, L (September 10, 1953), 421. The quotation is from Benjamin Rowland's *The Art and Architecture of India*.
21. "The Gods of India," 338.
22. See Glen O. Allen who, in "Structure, Symbol, and Theme in

A Passage to India," *PMLA,* LXX (December, 1955), identifies "Mosque" with emotion, "Caves" with intellect, and "Temple" with love. See Stone's discussion of "triads," 311–17.

23. The life of the goddess Vishnu furnishes a pattern for the events chronicled in the book and follows the same "seasonal" organization. See Stone, 309n.

24. This statement answers Crews' judgment, 142, that unity cannot be obtained. It can be sporadically experienced, but rather through disorder than through logic and harmony. Hinduism does not so much sacrifice the values of humanism (Crews, 150) as go beyond them.

25. "The Indian Mind," *New Weekly,* I (March 28, 1914), 55.

26. Crews' statement, 131, that the quest for meaning in the book is futile or ridiculous is, I think, extreme.

27. "Pessimism in Literature," *Working Men's College Journal,* X (January, 1907), 10.

28. "The Gods of India," 338.

29. See Edwin M. Moseley, *Pseudonyms of Christ in the Modern Novel* (Pittsburgh, 1962); Dauner; and Stone, 312–15.

Chapter Six

1. "E. M. Forster," *Kenyon Review,* V (1943), 621.

2. Thomson's archetypal characters include Gino Carella, Mr. Emerson, Lucy Honeychurch, Stephen Wonham, Rickie Elliot, Stewart Ansell, Mrs. Elliot, Robert, Mrs. Failing, Ruth Wilcox, Helen and Margaret Schlegel (in part), Professor Godbole, the courtroom punkah-wallah, Mrs. Moore, Ralph Moore, and Stella Moore.

Selected Bibliography

* PRIMARY SOURCES

1. *Novels*

All the novels appear in the Uniform Edition (London: Edward Arnold and Co., 1924) and in the Pocket Edition (London: Edward Arnold and Co. [1947]). The latter edition is still in print. Throughout the bibliography I list mainly the first English and American editions and available reprints. For other editions, consult Kirkpatrick's *Bibliography.*

Where Angels Fear to Tread. Edinburgh and London: William Blackwood and Sons, 1905; New York: Alfred A. Knopf, 1922;* New York: Vintage Books, 1958; Harmondsworth: Penguin Books, 1959.

The Longest Journey. Edinburgh and London: William Blackwood and Sons, 1907; New York: Alfred A. Knopf, 1922; Harmondsworth: Penguin Books, 1960; London and New York: Oxford University Press ("World Classics Edition"), 1960 with Introduction by E. M. FORSTER;* New York: Vintage Books, 1962.

A Room with a View. London: Edward Arnold and Co., 1908; New York and London: G. P. Putnam's Sons, 1911; Harmondsworth: Penguin Books, 1955;* New York: Vintage Books, 1960.

Howards End. London: Edward Arnold and Co., 1910; New York and London: G. P. Putnam's Sons, 1910; Harmondsworth: Penguin Books, 1950;* New York: Vintage Books, 1954.

A Passage to India. London: Edward Arnold and Co., 1924; New York: Harcourt, Brace and Co., 1924; London: J. M. Dent and Sons ("Everyman's Library"), 1942, revised 1957 with Foreword and Author's Notes by E. M. FORSTER; Harmondsworth: Penguin Books, 1950;* New York: Harbrace Modern Classics, 1958, and Harvest Books [1965] (pagination is identical in 1958 and 1965 editions).

* Asterisks indicate editions referred to in this study.

149

2. Short Stories

The Celestial Omnibus and Other Stories. London: Sidgwick and Jackson, 1911; New York: Alfred A. Knopf, 1923.

The Eternal Moment and Other Stories. London: Sidgwick and Jackson, 1928; New York: Harcourt, Brace and Co., 1928; New York: Grosset's Universal Library, 1964.

* *The Collected Tales of E. M. Forster.* New York: Alfred A. Knopf, 1947.

Collected Short Stories of E. M. Forster. London: Sidgwick and Jackson, 1948; Harmondsworth: Penguin Books, 1954.

3. Other Books of Prose

Alexandria: A History and a Guide. Alexandria: Whitehead Morris, 1922; * Garden City: Doubleday and Co. (Anchor Books), 1961, with an Introduction by E. M. FORSTER.

Pharos and Pharillon. Richmond: Leonard and Virginia Woolf, 1923; New York: Alfred A. Knopf, 1923 (* reissued, 1962).

Aspects of the Novel. London: Edward Arnold and Co., 1927; New York: Harcourt, Brace and Co., 1927. Reprinted in Pocket Edition (London, 1949); Harbrace Modern Classics (New York, 1949); * Harvest Books (New York [1956]); and Penguin Books (Harmondsworth, 1962).

Goldsworthy Lowes Dickinson. London: Edward Arnold and Co., 1934; * New York: Harcourt, Brace and Co., 1934. Reprinted in Pocket Edition (London, 1962).

Abinger Harvest. London: Edward Arnold and Co., 1936; New York: Harcourt, Brace and Co., 1936. Reprinted in Pocket Edition (London, 1953) and * Harvest Books (New York [1967]). Reprints some of Forster's important essays, reviews, and miscellaneous works.

England's Pleasant Land, a Pageant Play. London: The Hogarth Press, 1940.

Nordic Twilight. London: Macmillan and Co. ("Macmillan War Pamphlet"), 1940. Similar to "Three Anti-Nazi Broadcasts," *Two Cheers for Democracy.*

Billy Budd: an Opera in Four Acts. Libretto by E. M. Forster and Eric Crozier, Adapted from the Story by Herman Melville. London and New York: Boosey and Hawkes, 1951; revised version, 1962.

Two Cheers for Democracy. London: Edward Arnold and Co., 1951; New York: Harcourt, Brace and Co., 1951. Reprinted in * Harvest Books (New York [1962]). Reprints other essays, reviews, and miscellaneous works.

The Hill of Devi. London: Edward Arnold and Co., 1953; * New York: Harcourt, Brace and Co., 1953.

Marianne Thornton (1797–1887): A Domestic Biography. London: Edward Arnold and Co., 1956; * New York: Harcourt, Brace and Co., 1956.

4. Miscellaneous Writings

(1) Pamphlets and Contributions to Books. Forster wrote several pamphlets which were mostly reprinted in *Two Cheers for Democracy.* He also contributed chapters or introductions to many books. For all these items, see B. J. Kirkpatrick's *Bibliography.*

(2) Uncollected Essays, Reviews, and Letters in Periodicals and Newspapers. These are numerous and important for understanding Forster. He has collected only a portion of them in *Abinger Harvest* and *Two Cheers for Democracy.* For a full listing, see B. J. Kirkpatrick's *Bibliography.*

SECONDARY SOURCES

In this selected list I include all book-length studies and important interviews, and the indispensable articles.

ALLEN, GLEN O. "Structure, Symbol, and Theme in *A Passage to India*," *PMLA*, LXX (December, 1955), 934–54. Provocative if overschematized discussion; offers a Hindu interpretation of Mrs. Moore's experiences in the Marabar Caves.

ALLEN, WALTER. *The English Novel.* New York: Dutton, 1955. Informed, judicious treatment. Similar discussion appears in *The Modern Novel in Britain and the United States.* New York: Dutton, 1964.

————. "Reassessments—*Howards End*," *New Statesman and Nation*, XLIX (March 19, 1955), 407–8. Challenging, closely reasoned essay.

AULT, PETER. "Aspects of E. M. Forster," *Dublin Review*, CCIX (October, 1946), 109–34. Exacting critique; centers on Forster's alleged inability to define precisely his values and visionary moments.

AUSTIN, EDGAR A. "Rites of Passage in *A Passage to India*," *Orient/West* (IX, iii, 1964), 64–72. Traces influence of Cambridge anthropologists over Forster. Mrs. Moore is a sacrificial god, whose powers are genuine but limited.

BEEBE, MAURICE and BROGUNIER, JOSEPH. "Criticism of E. M. Forster: a Selected Checklist," *Modern Fiction Studies*, VII (Autumn, 1961), 284–92. Lists secondary works.

BEER, J. B. *The Achievement of E. M. Forster*. London: Chatto and
Windus; New York: Barnes and Noble, 1962. Sees Forster's fiction as uniting three main impulses: social comedy or realism,
moral commitment, and Romantic vision; discursive and quotes
too much, but provides sensitive readings of the novels.

BELGION, MONTGOMERY. "The Diabolism of E. M. Forster," *Criterion*,
XIV (October, 1934), 54–73. Incisive essay; finds that Forster's
rich talent and his questionable values are "diabolical" in combi-
nation.

BELL, QUENTIN. *Bloomsbury*. ("Pageant of History" series.) London:
Weidenfeld and Nelson, 1968. Excellent discussion of Bloomsbury
by one who knows it from the inside.

BENTLEY, PHYLLIS. "The Novels of E. M. Forster," *College English*,
IX (April, 1948), 349–56. Appreciative essay; attentive to
Forster's artistry.

BERLAND, ALWYN. "James and Forster: The Morality of Class," *Cambridge Journal*, VI (February, 1953), 259–80. Perceptively com-
pares "the pastoral" *Howards End* with James's "civilized" novels.

BOWEN, ELIZABETH. "E. M. Forster." *Collected Impressions*. New York:
Alfred A. Knopf, 1950. Vigorous treatment of Forster's miscellaneous prose, his characters, his style, and his mind.

BRADBURY, MALCOLM. "E. M. Forster's *Howards End*," *Critical Quarterly*, IV (Autumn, 1962), 229–41. Excellent essay; stresses
Forster's broad vision which includes a comic mode concerned
with social commentary and a poetic mode concerned with moral
and spiritual values. Revised form of essay in book cited in next
entry.

———. (Ed.) *Forster: A Collection of Critical Essays*. ("Twentieth
Century Views.") Englewood Cliffs, New Jersey: Prentice-Hall,
1966. Introduction is an illuminating survey of Forster's literary
reputation and of tendencies in recent Forster criticism. In general, American critics regard Forster as writer of symbolic romance;
British critics, as comic and realistic novelist. Good collection of
standard essays on Forster.

BRANDER, LAURENCE. *E. M. Forster: A Critical Study*. London: Rupert
Hart-Davis, 1968. Impressionistic account, disappointing in its
lack of critical insight and its reliance on plot summaries.

BREIT, HARVEY. "E. M. Forster," *The Writer Observed*. Cleveland:
World Publishing Co., 1956. Interview with Forster, first published in *New York Times Book Review*, June 14, 1949. Forster
discusses Joyce, George Eliot, and the "civilized" Matthew Arnold.

BROWER, REUBEN A. "The Twilight of the Double Vision: Symbol and
Irony in *A Passage to India*." *The Fields of Light*. New York: Ox-

ford University Press, 1951. Standard essay; sees the book's pattern in terms of the mosque-arch-night, cave-echo-heat, and temple-sky-rain metaphors. Finds Mrs. Moore's disillusion in "Caves" more effective than the affirmations made in "Temple."

BROWN, E. K. "E. M. Forster and the Contemplative Novel," *University of Toronto Quarterly*, III (April, 1934), 349–61. Stresses "the chasm between the world of actions and the world of being" and the importance of "visionary" characters in the novels.

———. "Expanding Symbols" and "Rhythm in E. M. Forster's *A Passage to India." Rhythm in the Novel*. Toronto: University of Toronto Press, 1950. Discusses Forster's rhythms: the recurring symbol, the expanding symbol, and interweaving themes. Excellent discussion of image patterns.

BURRA, PETER. "The Novels of E. M. Forster," *Nineteenth Century and After*, CXVI (November, 1935), 581–94. Reprinted as Introduction to Everyman's edition of *A Passage to India* (London: J. M. Dent and Sons, 1942). Early essay and one of the best; stresses the complexities of Forster's vision.

CECIL, DAVID. "E. M. Forster." *Poets and Story Tellers*. New York: Macmillan, 1949. Stimulating essay; emphasizes subtlety of Forster's art and characters, and his occasional failures.

CHURCHILL, THOMAS. "Place and Personality in *Howards End*," *Critique*, V (Spring–Summer, 1962), 61–73. Trenchant account, stressing superiority of Mrs. Wilcox both to her immediate family and to the Schlegels.

COX, C. B. "E. M. Forster's Island." *The Free Spirit: A Study of Liberal Humanism in the Novels of George Eliot, Henry James, E. M. Forster, Virginia Woolf, Angus Wilson*. London and New York: Oxford University Press, 1963. Critical analysis of Forster's liberal humanism, especially his imputed failure to relate it to social reality.

CREWS, FREDERICK C. *E. M. Forster: The Perils of Humanism*. Princeton: Princeton University Press, 1962. Indispensable both for generalizations about Forster's place in intellectual history and for brilliant criticism of the novels. Overstresses pessimism, I think, of *A Passage to India*. By now a standard work.

DALESKI, H. M. "Rhythmic and Symbolic Patterns in *A Passage to India." Studies in English Language and Literature*, XVII, ed. ALICE SHALVI and A. A. MENDILOW. Jerusalem: The Hebrew University, 1966. Original and provocative discussion, stressing cyclic aspects of *A Passage to India*.

DAUNER, LOUISE. "What Happened in the Cave? Reflections on *A Passage to India," Modern Fiction Studies*, VII (Autumn, 1961),

258–70. Well-reasoned interpretation. The Marabar Caves include the poles of life and death, unity and separateness, and are related to Plato's caves, the Hindu concept of Maya, and Kali, the Great Mother.

ENRIGHT, D. J. "To the Lighthouse or to India." *The Apothecary's Shop: Essays on Literature.* London: Secker and Warburg, 1957. Forster achieves a balance between outer and inner experience in *A Passage to India* that eludes Mrs. Woolf in *To the Lighthouse.*

FURBANK, P. N. and HASKELL, F. J. H. *Writers at Work, The Paris Review Interviews,* ed. MALCOLM COWLEY. New York: Viking Press, 1958. Indispensable for Forster's remarks upon characters and technical problems in writing his novels.

GERBER, HELMUT E. (ed.). "E. M. Forster; an Annotated Checklist of Writings about Him," *English Fiction in Transition,* II, i (1959), 4–27, and following issues. Annotated continuous listings of secondary materials. I have done annotations since 1966.

GODFREY, DENIS. *E. M. Forster's Other Kingdom.* Edinburgh and London: Oliver and Boyd; New York: Barnes and Noble, 1968. Thin and superficial study, discussing novels on the basis of plot summaries and inadequate philosophical premises.

GRANSDEN, K. W. "E. M. Forster at Eighty," *Encounter,* XII (January, 1959), 77–81. Article based on interview with Forster.

————. *E. M. Forster.* Edinburgh and London: Oliver and Boyd ("Writers and Critics"); New York: Grove Press (Evergreen Pilot Books), 1962. Survey; stronger in its analysis of individual novels than in its generalizations.

HALL, JAMES. "Forster's Family Reunions." *The Tragic Comedians.* Bloomington: Indiana University Press, 1963. Penetrating essay; concentrates on *Howards End* and the family as a means of preserving a vital tradition.

HANNAH, DONALD. "The Limitations of Liberalism in E. M. Forster's Work," *English Miscellany,* XIII (1962), 165–78. Maintains that the stature of *A Passage to India* depends on Forster's recognition in it of the limitations of liberalism whereas he had failed to face them squarely in *Howards End.* Stimulating though arbitrary discussion.

HARDY, BARBARA. "Dogmatic Form: Defoe, Charlotte Bronte, Thomas Hardy, and E. M. Forster." *The Appropriate Form: An Essay on the Novel.* London: University of London (Athlone Press), 1964. Maintains that Forster's liberalism, though undogmatic, imposes too rigid a form upon the novels.

HARDY, JOHN EDWARD. "*Howards End:* The Sacred Center." *Man in the Modern Novel.* Seattle: University of Washington Press, 1964.

Judicious essay; sees *Howards End* as stressing the theme of integrity and dramatizing the divisions in modern life.

HARVEY, JOHN. "Imagination and Moral Theme in E. M. Forster's *The Longest Journey*," *Essays in Criticism*, VI (October, 1956), 418–33. Rigorous treatment of the novel's inadequacies.

HAWORTH, HERBERT. "E. M. Forster and the Contrite Establishment," *Journal of General Education*, XVII (October, 1965), 190–206. Informative article which traces some of Forster's ideas to his friends on the editorial staff of the liberal *Independent Review* and to the *Review* itself.

HOFFMAN, FREDERICK J. "*Howards End* and the Bogey of Progress," *Modern Fiction Studies*, VII (Autumn, 1961), 243–57. Able discussion of *Howards End* as critique of Edwardian "progress." Partly reprinted in *The Mortal No* (Princeton: University Press, 1964).

HOLLINGSWORTH, KEITH. "*A Passage to India*: the Echoes in the Marabar Caves," *Criticism*, IV (Summer, 1962), 210–24. Succinct analysis; the "cave" experiences represent communication stopped and love denied for Adela Quested and Mrs. Moore.

HOLROYD, MICHAEL. *Lytton Strachey*. Vol. I: *The Unknown Years 1880–1920*. London: Heinemann, 1967; New York: Holt, Rinehart and Winston, 1968. Vol. II: *The Years of Achievement 1910–1932*. London: Heinemann; New York: Holt, Rinehart and Winston, 1968. Forster often figures in this monumental biography. Of prime importance also for the Bloomsbury background.

HOLT, LEE E. "E. M. Forster and Samuel Butler," *PMLA*, LXI (September, 1946), 804–19. Discerning essay.

HOROWITZ, ELLIN. "The Communal Ritual and the Dying God in E. M. Forster's *A Passage to India*," *Criticism*, VI (Winter, 1964), 70–88. Astute interpretation; stresses death-and-resurrection pattern embodied in Mrs. Moore.

HOY, CYRUS. "Forster's Metaphysical Novel," *PMLA*, LXXV (March, 1960), 126–36. Sensitive reading of *Howards End* with many sharp insights and some questionable conclusions; stresses struggle between yeoman heritage of Ruth Wilcox and imperialism represented by her family.

HYNES, SAMUEL. "Forster at Eighty-Five: The Old Man at King's," *Commonweal*, LXXIX (February 21, 1964), 635–38. Important essay; maintains that Forster's liberal humanism has supported his personal life but has not been able to support continued creativity.

JOHNSTONE, J. K. *The Bloomsbury Group: A Study of E. M. Forster, Lytton Strachey, Virginia Woolf, and Their Circle*. New York:

Noonday Press, 1954. Valuable for Forster's background in the Cambridge of G. E. Moore and in the Bloomsbury Group.

JONES, DAVID. "E. M. Forster on His Life and His Books," *Listener,* LXI (January 1, 1959), 11–12. Important interview.

JONES, E. B. C. "E. M. Forster and Virginia Woolf." *The English Novelists,* ed. DEREK VERSCHOYLE. London: Chatto and Windus, 1936. General discussion still of value.

JOSEPH, DAVID I. *The Art of Rearrangement: E. M. Forster's "Abinger Harvest."* New Haven: Yale University Press, 1964. Detailed but superficial analysis of the themes, organization, and artistry revealed in *Abinger Harvest.*

KARL, FREDERICK R. and MAGALANER, MARVIN. "E. M. Forster." *A Reader's Guide to Great Twentieth Century English Novels.* New York: The Noonday Press, 1959. Persuasive analysis of *Where Angels Fear to Tread, Howards End,* and *A Passage to India.*

KEIR, W. A. S. "*A Passage to India* Reconsidered," *Cambridge Journal,* V (April, 1952), 426–35. Argues that the power of the novel depends on its symbolic suggestiveness.

KELVIN, NORMAN. *E. M. Forster.* Carbondale and Edwardsville: Southern Illinois University Press, 1967. Inadequate book to appear at this late date.

KERMODE, FRANK. "Mr. E. M. Forster as a Symbolist," *Listener,* LIX (January 2, 1958), 17–18. Reprinted as "The One Orderly Product." *Puzzles and Epiphanies, Essays and Reviews, 1958–1961.* New York: Chilmark Press, 1962. Maintains that Forster's esthetic is mainly symbolist.

KIRKPATRICK, B. J. *A Bibliography of E. M. Forster.* ("The Soho Bibliographies," XIX.) London: Rupert Hart-Davis, 1965; second edition, 1968. Meticulously compiled bibliography of Forster's collected and uncollected works. Standard and indispensable.

KLINGOPULOS, G. D. "E. M. Forster's Sense of History and Cavafy," *Essays in Criticism,* VIII (April, 1958), 156–65. Maintains that Forster's perspectives were enlarged after 1910 by a more comprehensive view of Hellenism and history than he had revealed in the early books.

———. "Mr. Forster's Good Influence." *The Modern Age* (*The Pelican Guide to English Literature,* Vol. VII). Harmondsworth (Sussex) and Baltimore: Penguin Books, 1961. Incisive account; celebrates Forster both as public commentator and as artist.

LANGBAUM, ROBERT. "A New Look at E. M. Forster," *Southern Review,* IV (Winter, 1968), 33–49. Challenging essay with many useful insights, focusing on *Where Angels Fear to Tread* and *A Passage to India* as Forster's masterpieces.

LEAVIS, F. R. "E. M. Forster," *Scrutiny,* VII (September, 1938), 185–

202. Also in *The Common Pursuit*. London: Chatto and Windus; New York: George W. Stewart, 1952. Germinal if somewhat rigid treatment of Forster's work.

LUCAS, JOHN. "Wagner and Forster: *Parsifal* and *A Room with a View*," *English Literary History* (March, 1966), 92–117. Interesting but discursive essay showing Forster's use of music in his novels; traces *Parsifal* analogues in *A Room with a View*.

MACAULAY, ROSE. *The Writings of E. M. Forster*. London: The Hogarth Press; New York: Harcourt, Brace and Co., 1938. Initial full-length study; somewhat relaxed, but still valuable for details of Forster's career, discussion of his uncollected work, and comment on his characters.

MAGNUS, JOHN. "Ritual Aspects of E. M. Forster's *The Longest Journey*," *Modern Fiction Studies*, XIII (Summer, 1967), 195–210. Germinal essay defining the rituals used in *The Longest Journey* for structural and thematic purposes.

McCONKEY, JAMES. *The Novels of E. M. Forster*. Ithaca: Cornell University Press, 1957. Illuminating book; emphasizes too much the role of the Forsterian "voice"; excellent on characters, symbols, and *A Passage to India*.

McDOWELL, FREDERICK P. W. " 'The Mild, Intellectual Light': Idea and Theme in *Howards End*," *PMLA*, LXXIV (September, 1959), 453–63. This essay and those that follow contain some materials additional to those found in this book.

———. "Forster's Many-Faceted Universe: Idea and Paradox in *The Longest Journey*," *Critique*, IV (Fall–Winter, 1960–61), 41–63.

———. "Forster's 'Natural Supernaturalism': The Tales," *Modern Fiction Studies*, VII (Autumn, 1961), 271–83.

———. "The Newest Elucidations of Forster," *English Fiction in Transition*, V, No. 4 (1962), 51–58.

———. "Forster's Most Recent Critics," *English Literature in Transition*, VII, No. 1 (1965), 49–60.

———. "E. M. Forster's Conception of the Critic," *Tennessee Studies in Literature*, X (1965), 93–100.

———. "E. M. Forster: Recent Extended Studies," *English Literature in Transition*, X, No. 3 (1966), 156–68.

———. "E. M. Forster's Theory of Literature," *Criticism*, VIII (Winter, 1966), 19–43.

MOORE, HARRY T. *E. M. Forster* ("Columbia Essays on Modern Writers"). New York: Columbia University Press, 1965. Readable survey of Forster's life and work.

MOSELEY, EDWIN M. "Christ as One Avatar: E. M. Forster's *A Passage to India*." *Pseudonyms of Christ in the Modern Novel*. Pittsburgh: University of Pittsburgh Press, 1962. Suggests Mrs. Moore is a goddess figure, corresponding to Kali, the Great Mother; also suggests parallel between Christ and Krishna as death-resurrection symbols.

————. "A New Correlative for *Howard End:* Demeter and Persephone," *Lock Haven Bulletin*, Series I, No. 3 (1961), 1–6. Suggests some parallels from Greek mythology for the characters.

NATWAR-SINGH, K. (ed.). *E. M. Forster: A Tribute. With Selections from His Writings on India.* New York: Harcourt, Brace and World, 1964. Appreciative essays by Forster's Indian disciples, revealing his far-reaching influence in the East. Includes some of Forster's writings on India, an interview, and his tribute to Gandhi.

NIERENBERG, EDWIN. "The Withered Priestess: Mrs. Moore's Incomplete Passage to India," *Modern Language Quarterly*, XXV (June, 1964), 198–204. Attempts, inconclusively, to refute the view of Mrs. Moore as a redemptive influence.

————. "The Prophecy of E. M. Forster," *Queen's Quarterly*, LXXI (Summer, 1964), 189–202. Able presentation of Forster's philosophy and religious values. Extended analysis of "The Story of the Siren."

O'CONNOR, WILLIAM VAN. "Toward a History of Bloomsbury," *Southwest Review*, XL (Winter, 1955), 36–52. Most succinct account of Bloomsbury and Forster's place therein.

OLIVER, H. J. *The Art of E. M. Forster.* Melbourne: Melbourne University Press, 1960. Sound though not brilliant study of the fiction.

PAINTER-DOWNES, MOLLIE. "Kingsman," *New Yorker*, XXXV (September 19, 1959), 51–86. "Profile" of Forster; valuable for insights into his personality and present values.

PEDERSON, GLENN. "Forster's Symbolic Form," *Kenyon Review*, XXI (Spring, 1959), 231–49. Suggestive, if discursive, treatment of *A Passage to India.*

PRITCHETT, V. S. "Mr. Forster's Birthday," *The Living Novel and Later Appreciations.* New York: Random House, 1964. Penetrating appraisal of Forster's spiritual significance for the modern age.

RANSOM, JOHN CROWE. "E. M. Forster," *Kenyon Review*, V (Autumn, 1943), 618–23. Early but still illuminating essay; emphasizes Forster's "benevolent anarchism," the beauty of his style, his depth of vision, and his distinction as a landscape poet.

RICHARDS, I. A. "A Passage to Forster," *Forum*, LXXVIII (December, 1927), 914–29. Early but still valuable treatment of Forster's world-view and his fiction; discusses *Howards End* as his most representative book.

RUECKERT, WILLIAM H. *Kenneth Burke and the Drama of Human Relations.* Minneapolis: University of Minnesota Press, 1963. Excellent analysis of dialectical patterns in *A Passage to India* and of symbolism in *Howards End*.

SAVAGE, DEREK S. "E. M. Forster." *The Withered Branch: Six Studies in the Modern Novel*. New York: Pellegrini and Cudahy, 1952. Unsympathetic critique of Forster's "confused" liberalism.

SHAHANE, V. A. *E. M. Forster: A Reassessment*. Delhi: Kitab Mahal, 1962. Perfunctory survey.

SHAHANE, V. A. (ed.). *Perspectives on E. M. Forster's 'A Passage to India': A Collection of Critical Essays*. New York: Barnes and Noble, 1968. A collection of standard essays on *A Passage to India* and a few substandard ones.

SHUSTERMAN, DAVID. *The Quest for Certitude in E. M. Forster's Fiction*. Bloomington: Indiana University Press, 1965. Sees Forster as the victim of conflict between impulses taking him to the world and those taking him to art. Shallow book; its presentation of Godbole as an evil man is eccentric and unwarranted.

SMITH, H. A. "Forster's Humanism and the Nineteenth Century." *Forster: A Collection of Critical Essays*, ed. MALCOLM BRADBURY. Englewood Cliffs, New Jersey: Prentice-Hall, 1966. Perceptive essay, showing that bourgeois Sawston is opposed by two "humanisms," a Romantic, intuitive one and a rational, intellectual one.

SPENCE, JONATHAN. "E. M. Forster at Eighty," *New Republic*, CLXI (October 5, 1959), 17–21. Stimulating reappraisal; emphasizes positive aspects of Forster's vision.

SPENDER, STEPHEN. "Personal Relations and Public Powers." *The Creative Element: a Study of Vision, Despair, and Orthodoxy among Some Modern Writers*. London: Hamish Hamilton, 1953. Challenging essay; analyzes Forster's values and their vital if provisional nature.

STALLYBRASS, OLIVER (ed.). *Aspects of E. M. Forster: Essays and Recollections Written for His Ninetieth Birthday January 1, 1969*. London: Edward Arnold; New York: Harcourt, Brace and World, 1969. Significant essays, biographical, critical, and reminiscent by some of Forster's friends and critics, including Elizabeth Bowen, Patrick Wilkinson, David Garnett, K. Natwar-Singh, Alec Randall, Willliam Roerick, W. J. H. Sprott, Benjamin Britten, John Arlott, B. W. Fagan, William Plomer, Wilfred Stone, Malcolm Bradbury, Oliver Stallybrass, and George H. Thomson.

STONE, WILFRED. *The Cave and the Mountain: A Study of E. M. Forster*. Stanford: Stanford University Press, 1966. Compendious book, full of valuable information and insights. Psychological approach to the fiction sometimes results in distortions, but critique of *A Passage to India* is masterly.

SWINNERTON, FRANK. *The Georgian Scene*. New York: Farrar and Rinehart, 1934. Judicious appraisal of Forster's novels and his qualities as writer.

THOMAS, ROY and HOWARD ERSKINE-HILL. "A Passage to India: Two Points of View," *Anglo-Welsh Review*, XV (Summer, 1965), 44–46, 46–50. Interesting essays on *A Passage to India*.

THOMSON, GEORGE H. *The Fiction of E. M. Forster*. Detroit: Wayne State University Press, 1967. Brilliant study of the symbolical and archetypal aspects of E. M. Forster's fiction. Astute and acute book, first-class in every respect, and soon should become standard. Includes much of the material present in Thomson's earlier articles on Forster.

TINDALL, WILLIAM YORK. *The Literary Symbol*. New York: Columbia University Press, 1955. Discussion of the caves in *A Passage to India* and Leonard Bast's death in *Howards End*.

————. *Forces in Modern British Literature, 1885–1946*. New York: Alfred A. Knopf, 1947. Incidental but incisive discussions of the novels and some of the tales.

TOYNBEE, PHILIP. "E. M. Forster at Eighty," *Observer* (December 20, 1958), pp. 8, 10. Important interview.

TRAVERSI, D. A. "The Novels of E. M. Forster," *Arena*, I (April, 1937), 28–40. Searching commentary; stresses Forster's aim of achieving mediation of extremes and his partial failure to do so.

TRILLING, LIONEL. *E. M. Forster*. ("The Makers of Modern Literature.") Norfolk, Connecticut: New Directions, 1943 (second edition, 1964); London: The Hogarth Press, 1944. Pioneer study; analyzes Forster both as liberal humanist and as artist. Valuable more for esthetic than for political and philosophical judgments; Trilling's doctrinaire liberalism obtrudes too greatly.

VOORHEES, RICHARD J. "The Novels of E. M. Forster." *South Atlantic Quarterly*, LIII (January, 1954), 89–99. Informed and perceptive essay.

WAGGONER, HYATT HOWE. "Exercises in Perspective: Notes on the Use of Coincidence in the Novels of E. M. Forster," *Chimera*, III (Summer, 1945), 3–14. Impressive essay; suggests that the coincidences and sudden deaths are not so much violations as extensions of our sense of reality.

WARNER, REX. *E. M. Forster*. ("Writers and Their Work," No. 7.) London: Longmans Green, 1950. Revised 1954 and 1960. Also available in *British Writers and Their Work No. 3*. Lincoln: University of Nebraska Press, 1964. Informed, lucid survey.

WARREN, AUSTIN. "The Novels of E. M. Forster," *American Review*, IX (Summer, 1937), 226–51. Also in *Rage for Order*. Chicago:

University of Chicago Press, 1948. Intelligent discussion, especially of Forster's values and naturalistic humanism.

WATTS, STEPHEN. "Forster on 'India'—Author Talks about Novel-into-Play," *New York Times,* January 28, 1962, Sec. 2, pp. 1, 3. Interesting interview.

WERRY, RICHARD R. "Rhythm in Forster's *A Passage to India,*" *Wayne State University: Studies in Honor of John Wilcox,* ed. A. DAYLE WALLACE and WOODBURN O. ROSS. Detroit: Wayne State University Press, 1958. Discussion of "easy" and "difficult" rhythms in the novel.

WESTBURG, BARRY R. "Forster's Fifth Symphony: Another Aspect of *Howards End,*" *Modern Fiction Studies,* X (Winter, 1964–65), 359–65. Interesting discussion; Helen Schlegel interprets the arts in terms of one another and of her personal experience.

WHITE, GERTRUDE M. "*A Passage to India:* Analysis and Revaluation," *PMLA,* LXVIII (December, 1953), 641–57. Standard essay; stresses the separation-reconciliation patterns and the "dialectical" organization of the novel.

WILDE, ALAN. *Art and Order: A Study of E. M. Forster.* New York: New York University Press, 1964. Perceptive book on Forster's fiction; alleges that Forster searched for order but was increasingly unable to find it in the social world or to mirror it in art.

WILSON, ANGUS. "A Conversation with E. M. Forster," *Encounter,* IX (November, 1957), 52–57. Important interview.

WOOLF, LEONARD. *Sowing: An Autobiography of the Years 1880 to 1904.* London: Hogarth Press; New York: Harcourt, Brace and World, 1960.

———. *Growing: An Autobiography of the Years 1904 to 1911.* London: Hogarth Press, 1961; New York: Harcourt, Brace and World, 1962.

———. *Beginning Again: An Autobiography of the Years 1911 to 1918.* London: Hogarth Press; New York: Harcourt, Brace and World, 1964.

———. *Downhill All the Way: An Autobiography of the Years 1919 to 1939.* London: Hogarth Press; New York: Harcourt, Brace and World, 1967. Forster often figures in these books. Important for establishing the social and intellectual backgrounds out of which Forster wrote and for the insights they provide into Bloomsbury.

WOOLF, VIRGINIA. "The Novels of E. M. Forster," *Atlantic Monthly,* CXV (November, 1927), 642–48. Also in *The Death of the Moth.* New York: Harcourt, Brace and Co., 1942. Standard if severe essay; criticizes Forster for failure to achieve wholeness of vision.

ZABEL, MORTON D. "E. M. Forster, the Trophies of the Mind." *Craft and Character in Modern Fiction.* New York: Viking Press, 1957. Cursory discussion of Forster's world and values.

ZWERDLING, ALEX. "The Novels of E. M. Forster," *Twentieth Century Literature,* II (January, 1957), 171–81. Good review of Forster's fiction.

Index